TARISHI KHANNA

Corporate Cocktail

A HAPPY HIGH

This is a work of nonfiction. The events and the incidents mentioned in the book are true and real. However, some names and characteristics have been changed, some events have been compressed, and some dialogues have been recreated.

First Edition: December 2025
Printed in India

Printed at: Parksons Graphics
Typeset in Adobe Garamond

ISBN: 978-93-6070-073-7

Cover Design: Prajakta Sawant

STORYMIRROR
Stories that reflect you

Publisher: StoryMirror Infotech Pvt. Ltd.
Unit No-F/705, 7th Floor, Kailas Corporate Lounge,
Veer Savarkar Road, Vikhroli Park Site,
Vikhroli West, Mumbai-400079,
Maharashtra, India.

Web: storymirror.com
Facebook: @storymirror
Twitter: @story_mirror
Instagram: @storymirror
Email: marketing@storymirror.com

ACKNOWLEDGMENTS

Writing this book has been a journey of reflection, persistence, and unexpected joy. It began as an idea between chaotic work calls and weekend breaks, but it found its shape because of the people who stood by me-patiently, lovingly, and relentlessly.

To my husband Vishal Taneja-thank you for being my sounding board, my sanity check, and sometimes, my most brutal critic. For every few lines I wrote, you lent your ear-sometimes unwillingly, yet always thoughtfully. We debated, disagreed, and reworked paragraphs more times than I can count. But every word of yours, every timeline you nudged me to stick to, became the rhythm that carried this book forward. Your belief in me-even when I second-guessed myself-made all the difference.

To my parents, my in-laws, and my sister Ikanshi, thank you for cheering me on from afar. Just knowing you believed in the idea of this book gave me the emotional push to transform it from scattered notes into a tangible story. Your wisdom, your faith, and your constant check-ins meant more than I can ever articulate.

To my cat Chuski-thank you for being a quiet companion through it all. Your comforting presence, curled up beside my keyboard, was a reminder to pause, breathe, and just keep going.

To my book reviewers-thank you for being more than just a reader. You were the backbone, the tough cover of this book, holding it together when I questioned whether it was worth finishing. Your encouragement came at moments when I needed it the most, and your honesty gave this book its strength.

To the corporate family, thank you for being the place where my career, and this book, both found their roots. You gave me not just a job, but stories worth telling.

To my character Magh, thank you for becoming the mirror through which I could explore, express, and share the complexities of corporate life in a fun way. You are fictional, yet more real than I expected.

And lastly, to every reader picking up this book between back-to-back meetings or on a Sunday evening reset, thank you. I hope Corporate Cocktail brings you moments of recognition, relief, and maybe even a laugh or two. We're all figuring this out, one deck, one decision, one detour at a time.

Here's to the madness we call work, life, and balance-and the meaning we somehow find in it.

PREFACE

Dear readers,

In the corporate world, time is currency, and most of us are running short. We move from meetings to emails, from deadlines to deliverables, often with little room to pause. But somewhere between "EOD updates" and late-night deck reviews, a question inevitably bubbles up:

Why am I doing this?

Is this what I signed up for?

Should I update my LinkedIn or quit and start a café in the hills?

This book was born out of that pause.

Corporate Cocktail is not a manual, nor a memoir. It's a reflection-a blend of moments, milestones, and musings gathered over a decade in consulting, through roles big and small, across boardrooms and break rooms. It is shaped not only by my own journey at a consulting firm, but also by the countless conversations with colleagues, mentors, interns, clients, and even airport strangers curious enough to ask:

"How long do you plan to stay in consulting?"

"Do you ever disconnect?"

"Why are you carrying your laptop on a holiday?"

The answers lie somewhere in the pages that follow.

This book is for the interns quietly observing their first team call. For the managers trying to lead with empathy amidst chaos. For students wondering what life beyond a campus placement looks like. For anyone in a 9-to-infinity job questioning the trade-offs, the titles, and the to-do lists.

It is a space to laugh at the absurdities, reflect on the lessons, and perhaps reimagine what it means to grow in the world of work.

Inside, you'll find:

- Real stories of leadership without authority
- How the right people make a difference
- What makes people stay when the perks aren't enough
- And how some slides truly do change lives

While not every chapter may mirror your path, I hope the experiences shared spark a sense of familiarity, reassurance, or curiosity-whether you're just stepping into corporate corridors or have been walking them for years.

Because at the end of the day, corporate life may be chaotic, but with the right people and perspective, it can also be one hell of a cocktail.

Maybe it will even leave you with a happy high.

So, if you've time-boxed this book between your morning coffee and your next sync-up at work, let's take a sip?

TABLE OF CONTENTS

CHAPTER 1

THE FIRST JOB

"Welcome to ARC - Leading by example" - the bold letters on the induction board stood tall and unyielding just outside the glass - panelled room. The message, as strong as it was, didn't feel exaggerated to her. It felt real. Monumental. Like a gate to something much bigger than herself.

It was a blazing June afternoon in New Delhi, the kind where even the walls seemed to sweat and the city pulsed with restless energy. The sun beat down mercilessly on the roads, and the air was thick, almost syrupy with heat. Yet nothing could dampen her spirit today - not the weather, not the overcrowded metro, not even the fact that she'd been on the road for two hours. Because this wasn't just any other Monday. This was "Monday". Her first day at her dream workplace. Her first real job.

She stood for a moment outside the room, smoothing the front of her charcoal - grey suit - the one she'd bought with the money she earned tutoring kids after college hours. Every stitch of that fabric held a story: late nights preparing lesson plans, early mornings of bus rides across the city, juggling final - year projects with part - time work. It wasn't just a suit; it was her earned armor.

She stepped into the room with shoulders squared, eyes scanning the sleek interiors that smelled faintly of new carpet and ambition. The air conditioning offered relief from the heat outside, but the room buzzed with a different kind of pressure - the silent tension of first impressions and unspoken expectations.

Around her, other freshers were finding seats, murmuring introductions, eyes bright with both excitement and caution. And at the front of the room stood the instructor - a woman who exuded authority without trying.

She was tall, perhaps in her early forties, dressed in an impeccable navy - blue pantsuit, her posture as upright as a measuring stick. Her hair was tied back into a sleek bun, a silver ARC pin gleaming on her lapel. She didn't need to raise her voice to command attention. Her voice was calm but firm, her eyes sharp and observant, scanning each new recruit like a teacher who'd seen a thousand faces walk in and out, but still cared enough to learn every name.

When it was her turn, she took a deep breath, took three confident steps forward, and offered her hand with a composed smile.

"Magh Mehra," she said, her voice steady. It was a simple introduction, but to her, it felt like a declaration.

The instructor smiled back, a brief but approving look flashing in her eyes. "Welcome to ARC, Magh."

What followed was an eight - hour crash course in reality.

The room slowly filled with corporate - speak - KPIs, SLAs, value proposition, cross - functional teams - phrases that up until this morning had mostly lived in textbooks or LinkedIn posts. Now, they were her new grammar.

Magh sat up straighter, scribbling notes furiously as her mind struggled to grasp this new language. Yet, three phrases etched themselves into her memory - silent words, unspoken commandments that felt more powerful than speech:

"40-hour timesheet - conditions apply."

"Race the clock; meet the deadline."

"Client satisfaction is the key - no excuses."

No one explained the "conditions" on the timesheet. No one had to. The knowing chuckles from returning analysts seated at the back made the meaning clear. Forty hours was just a number on paper. In reality, time was elastic - and it often stretched late into the night.

The session didn't sugarcoat the truth. It wasn't about hand - holding. It was about aligning them with the larger machinery they were now part of - a well-oiled, fast-moving, client - centric ecosystem where excellence was expected, and excuses didn't have a place.

By the end of the day, the caffeine in the air had faded, the initial energy subsided into a quieter kind of focus. As the instructor clicked through the final slide, she paused, letting the room settle.

The screen glowed with a single line, stark against the white background:

"This is your own journey. It's your time to work with the clients to establish a long - lasting relationship with them."

She looked up once more, making eye contact with a few in the front row - including Magh - before walking out of the room, she said, "Good luck newcomers, welcome to ARC. Please collect your laptops from the IT room. Thank you."

Magh stayed seated a moment longer with a few others, her notebook open on the last page. Her pen hovered for a few seconds before she wrote, beneath her final note:

"The corporate race is on and this is where my story starts."

She was eager to unravel every word she grasped and delve deeper into it. The moment the induction concluded, she made her way to the IT room and collected her laptop. A resounding click from the mobile camera echoed, breaking the stillness of the IT room.

She wasted no time and posted the picture of her first office laptop in her family WhatsApp group. "Mummy Papa, see my office laptop. Just got it," she quoted in her post. She belonged to a middle - income group and she was the first of her generation to make the first move into the corporate world. Rather, she could have joined her family business of selling Indian suits and sarees like her other three cousins.

And there her journey began, with her first laptop, brimming with hope. Each key she pressed felt like a step forward, symbolizing the start of her dreams taking shape.

A month passed by, full of imagination weaving through her thoughts while she had been waiting to work on a client site. What this new life would offer besides the pay - check, what will I learn? What project will I get? When will I go to the client's place? How many more training sessions? What is this hustle bustle on the floor all the time? What are those meetings happening inside the partners' room? A series of unanswered questions that she kept looking for answers.

Her manager Saranya had assigned her training sessions, business proposals, where she could contribute to formatting CVs or help by adding images on the slides. There she read, for every client request for proposals (RFP), her managers were trying to give a perfect answer to match the client's expectations. How will they differentiate and why should the client choose them?

A thought struck her. While she was eager to develop business solutions, she never imagined that people's profiles would be a selling product with a price tag on it. To her amazement, people's profiles were offered at discounted and blended package rates.

There she noticed, with the solution that was planned for delivery, there was equal weight and attention given to the 'Our team' section too. It was too early to realize, but she felt that she would also be required to create her own placeholder in that section. For which she had to enter the race of never looking back - a trip to corporate consulting. The destination was not clear to her, but she found the start of the corporate - maze. She didn't know how many times she would be lost in the maze, what she wanted to achieve after crossing the maze, what roadblocks she would encounter on the way... All she knew was: there would be an endless streak of experiences.

She was learning the ins and outs of the corporate world each day and had countless questions on her mind and was puzzled most days at work. Some days she feared losing the race; some days she would pick herself up and navigate those answers by asking her managers over lunch or her peers during a quick morning catch - up. Sometimes she would patiently learn and keep her eyes and ears wide open to notice what her colleagues are up to.

On a day like no other, she attended a full - day training program on one of the key pieces of jargon she had been hearing almost every day at work - "Managing client expectations".

A week ago, when her outlook popped up with this invite, she had many questions about what the agenda would be.

Will this session answer all her queries? Will it help her to become succinct in delivering a client project independently?

Curiosity guiding her steps, she reached the training room at 9am sharp holding a Starbucks grande hot americano and a notebook. A series of placards lined the room, one of which evidently caught her attention, which said : Client is God! She laughed at first, being a spiritual girl, she thought there would be some wordplay in this statement.

Once the training kicked off, the instructor started sharing stories and tips about handling client expectations. A lot of it felt like theory - stuff you'd get better at with time and practice. But then he got serious and said, "For us, the client is like God. Just like people say the customer is king. So never ignore a call or email from them. Even if you can't fix the problem right away, you must reply immediately."

There was no wordplay for the next one hour.

All she knew was that she would find her own meaning in this, somewhere, someday!

On another busy day, she met him in the pantry where all the freshers used to hang out.

Navneet walked in, towering with a well-built frame that filled the doorway before he even spoke. His neatly tied navy - blue turban sat perfectly over his sharp features, giving him an air of effortless confidence. There was a calm strength in the way he moved - like someone used to being noticed but never demanding attention.

"How are you, Magh? Why are you in the office?" he asked in his deep, husky voice, the kind that sounded like it belonged to a TED Talk.

She chuckled, but before she could say anything, he grinned and jumped in.

"Let me tell you what my boss told me a decade ago," he said.

"He said, 'If you're a consultant and you're not working side-by-side with the client every day, then something's off. Around here, people start thinking you're just sitting on the bench, taking it easy - not really doing much.'"

The bench - a place known for free time in consulting. More time spent on the bench is inversely proportional to bonus money in your bank account.

As he entered the elevator, he concluded, "Next time we meet I hope to see you at a client's place."

The strong, unforgettable impression he had left during her interview hadn't faded - if anything, it had only grown stronger. Navneet wasn't just impressive on paper as an ARC partner; he embodied the kind of leader she had always hoped to work for - grounded, sharp, and quietly inspiring. But more than that, he was the kind of boss who didn't just lead from above; he walked beside you. He knew when to step in with a nudge, when to let you stumble and learn, and when to shield you from the blind spots you hadn't yet seen. His experience wasn't just a badge - it was a safety net, a compass, and a quiet push forward. With him, growth wasn't optional - it was inevitable.

As the elevator doors slid shut behind her with a quiet thud, she felt it - the next door in her corporate maze had just opened.

For the next 2 days, she tried to discuss with Saranya and other managers, but there were no client projects that she could be part of immediately. Every day, the response she got was "Don't worry there is a huge 'pipeline,' but currently new college joiners have no experience, so we can't assign you to any ongoing project. Client wants only experienced, confident, and technically strong resources. Go and do the training."

Being an impatient and overthinking Leo, she understood that waiting for a project is like losing time to grow in her career and delaying her 'planned timeline' to meet her dream goals.

Drawing from everything she'd absorbed in those first few months - through conversations with mentors, guidance from counselors, and feedback from managers - she made a strategic decision: to take on a mock project. It wasn't just about applying what she'd learned; it was about testing herself in a low-risk environment, building confidence, and preparing for the real challenges ahead.

Over the past four weeks, under Saranya's watchful yet encouraging eye, she and a teammate had been working on an idea - something small, but promising. Saranya stood barely five feet tall, but her presence filled the room. A Kashmiri by origin, she carried herself with quiet strength - rooted in high values, emotionally attuned to her team, yet always thinking three steps ahead.

She didn't micromanage; she nudged, she questioned, and she made sure they never lost sight of the bigger picture.

"I want you to own this," Saranya had said one afternoon, her tone firm but warm. "You've done the training. Now let's see how we can use it."

Motivated by that trust, Magh pulled together a short presentation - distilling everything she'd learned from her technical training sessions. It wasn't just slides; it was a pitch, a story, a glimpse of what she could bring to a real client. She presented it to Navneet with her other teammate, hoping to make an impression.

And just like she'd seen in other proposals, she crafted a one-pager - part resume, part sales pitch - for herself and her teammate. It highlighted their strengths, their skills, and the kind of value they could add to any project. It was her first attempt at selling not just an idea, but herself.

It was her first move to showcase that a college fresher comes with some experience, may not be technically strong or possess tactical management skills yet, but possesses a sharp mind full of ideas, an urge to learn, and the confidence to speak out her thoughts.

A few weeks later, both consultants landed a live client project with Saranya. Three months in, she ran into Navneet during a client meeting.

It felt like a full-circle moment.

He smiled, leaned in, and said with a knowing look, "Well done Magh. Keep it going."

But before she could thank him, his phone buzzed. He glanced at the screen and entered the nearby phone booth to take the call.

And just like that, he was gone - but his appreciation stuck with her. That day, something clicked. She knew this wasn't just about surviving the job. It was about learning the game, navigating the maze, and growing through every twist.

It was probably not an out-of-the-box thinking that helped her to move forward; it was the youthful impatience that drove her to navigate the pipeline diagonally.

Sound familiar? Like the story every newcomer had heard before, right?

Over lunch one afternoon, a few corporate veterans leaned back in their chairs, eyeing her and her teammate with amused curiosity.

"This is just the beginning," one of them said, half-smiling. "Let's see how long you will be motivated to step up."

It wasn't a threat, more like a rite of passage - a mix of challenge, warning, and welcome - all rolled into one.

She didn't flinch. She just nodded, quietly taking it in. The game had begun.

A few months into the project, the endless client chasers left her exhausted, her strength drained on every other day. She struggled to match the pace of the corporate hustle.

One evening, Magh stared at her screen, the deck finally complete. It was 8:15 p.m. The client floor had quieted down, but her mind hadn't. She leaned back, rubbing her eyes, unsure if she felt accomplished or just drained.

Just then, Saranya walked by, her steps light but purposeful. She paused at Magh's desk, noticing the open laptop and the tired eyes behind it.

"Dude, you're still here. You had a family dinner today. Didn't you?" Saranya asked, her voice soft but steady.

Magh nodded. "Just wrapped up the deck. Deadline's tomorrow morning."

Saranya pulled up a chair beside her. "You know, I've seen this look before. The 'I'm doing everything, but I'm not sure why' look."

Magh gave a tired smile. "Is it that obvious?"

Saranya chuckled. "Only to someone who's been through it. The first job feels like a rush, doesn't it? That spark when you get your first project, the thrill of being needed."

Magh nodded. "It does. But lately, it's like the timelines and the chaos are trying to snuff it out."

Saranya leaned in, her tone more reflective now. "That's the corporate rhythm. It pulls you in fast. But here's the thing

- don't let it define you. Learn to pause, to ask why you're doing what you're doing. That's how you grow."

Magh looked down at her screen. "I just don't want to lose that spark."

"You won't," Saranya said gently. "Not if you stay curious. Not if you remember that productivity isn't about staying late - it's about staying true to what you're learning."

She stood up, placing a hand lightly on Magh's shoulder. "Go home. Enjoy the family dinner. This isn't going anywhere. But your energy? That's yours to protect."

Magh watched her walk away, her words lingering like a quiet echo.

She shut her laptop, gathered her things, and took one last look at the empty floor.

This wasn't the end of the struggle. But maybe, just maybe - it was thc beginning of understanding it.

P.S. The first job is always special. That spark, that enthusiasm - it's real. But the corporate hustle will test it. If you've ever been a fresher, are about to join the corporate world, or have lived in it for years or you'll find a piece of yourself in the chapters ahead.

CHAPTER 2

NAVIGATING EXPECTATIONS

It was the summer of the Olympics in Rio de Janeiro. A stakeholder walked past in the client office where the team was celebrating the silver medal of PV Sindhu in badminton. "While India celebrates the victory, your deliverable timeline still stays the same", Rubesh said sarcastically. He was a middle-aged, tall, young man with brown eyes and long hair, which he never tied up. His personality spoke of years of experience with the firm, where he used to run tasks like the CEO of the firm. No one had the courage to challenge his opinions. Recently three employees had to quit due to his aggressive behavior, but he remained completely unfazed.

Right after his comments came to a close, all the teammates, except for the manager, returned to the work bay.

"The 5-minute celebration done by my team today will enhance their productivity for the next 5 hours at work," he said to the client. "As we are together for a longer and stronger partnership, I would like to say that such celebrations will happen quite often, but instead of a delay, I believe it will increase my team's motivation to work and will help to expedite the project delivery," he said.

A moment of silence with confident eye contact.

"I never wanted to engage talkers from consulting, but you are one of a kind, Taran. I acknowledge your honesty and how you find courage to fight for your team and never please me, but let me tell you my friend, this is not going to help you get any discount in the timeline. It is as firm as my words are," he responded, clenching his fists.

Taran replied with a warm smile. He made a remark, looking at his teammates, "We understand what a timeline means, Rubesh, never missed one because of the strength of teamwork we bring to the table. The last month's report was submitted 2 days before the timeline. I would appreciate it, if you valued the hard work of our team. Valuing efforts is priceless."

Rubesh smirked at his response and walked off, saying, "Water will be clear next week".

Curious, Magh walked over as soon as Taran returned to his desk.

He settled into his chair, his broad shoulders filling out a crisp white shirt tucked neatly into grey trousers. His hair was freshly cropped, and the black-framed glasses gave him a sharp, no-nonsense look. Even seated, he was tall enough that his eye level nearly matched hers.

Magh didn't wait. "So… isn't our client basically God?" she asked, half-serious. "Shouldn't we just do whatever he says and cancel all the celebrations from now on?"

Taran looked up, amused. "That's one way to put it," he said, adjusting his glasses. "But if you start worshipping every request, you'll burn out before the next billing cycle."

Another team member spoke up, a hint of concern in his voice. "But Taran… aren't you worried about escalation? What if the client pushes back and tightens the rules on us?"

Taran didn't respond right away. He leaned back in his chair, arms crossed, letting the silence stretch for a few seconds - long enough to make everyone lean in.

Then he said, calmly but firmly, "I've been where you are. A few years ago, I watched managers echo every word the client said - out of fear, not strategy. They followed blindly, thinking that was loyalty. But here's what I've learned: phrases like 'client is God' or 'customer is king' - they're often misunderstood."

He looked around the room, making sure his words landed.

"Yes, we listen to the client. Yes, we deliver. But that doesn't mean we switch off our judgment. I've learned to prioritize what the client needs and not just what they say. Sometimes, that means pushing back. Not to defy them, but to serve them better."

A few heads nodded. The room was quiet.

"This mindset won't win you points with every cutthroat manager," Taran continued. "But if you care about real productivity, about building teams that last, then you have to draw the line."

He stood up, voice steady.

"My mantra is simple: don't be a blind follower leading blind followers. Be the kind of leader who knows where the edge is, and isn't afraid to protect the team from falling off it. Your team is your biggest asset. If they're supported, if they're happy - there's nothing they can't deliver."

Everyone beamed, and in the blink of an eye, the room filled with the familiar clatter of laptop keys. The team had snapped back into work mode.

Then, an email popped up on Taran's screen.

No subject line could have stirred more tension.

The energy shifted. A few glanced around, sensing something was off. Whispers floated - some guessed it had to do with the earlier exchange between Taran and Rubesh. No one asked. No one confirmed. The silence was its own answer.

Taran stood abruptly, pushing back his chair. He limped slightly as he walked out, a detail few had noticed before. From the pantry door, he was seen on a call, wiping sweat from his brow. His posture was tense; his voice low. He looked… anxious.

Back at their desks, the team murmured in worry. What was in that email? What had happened?

But as the saying goes - some things are meant to be brushed under the carpet, never uncovered. The email became a quiet mystery. Taran never mentioned Rubesh again that day.

Instead, he returned with his usual fire, rallying the team with sharp focus and unwavering energy. He pushed them to finish strong, to stay sharp, to believe in the work.

It was the first day of the project that Taran didn't leave with the team.

He stayed back.

Until when?

No one knows. Not even now.

P.S. There's a lot it takes to be a manager - far more than what the team sees. Sometimes, it's the invisible armor they wear, shielding their people from chaos, quietly absorbing the blows. And most of the time, no one even knows it's there.

Just another day in the office grind. Magh and Taran sat stiffly, dreading the 9 a.m. meeting with Rubesh; he was known for his razor-sharp grip on numbers and zero tolerance for fluff too.

He walked into the room, and silence followed like a shadow.

It was Magh's first big meeting with him. Months of work were about to be laid bare. Rubesh, unexpectedly cordial, offered a firm handshake to Taran, then turned to Magh. Her hand trembled, but she steadied herself. The nerves returned as she fumbled with the projector setup. A few seconds later, the meeting began.

Taran took the lead, presenting the business outcomes of the sales forecast report that Magh and the team had built. The room was focused until Rubesh abruptly stood up.

"You consultants have no business knowledge," he snapped. "Your work is of no value to me or my team. The numbers may be correct, but your approach is completely off. Do you even realize how much I'm paying to outsource this?"

Magh instinctively opened her mouth to respond, and a voice cut through from behind.

"Rubesh, we've reviewed the numbers. Your team validated the data - they can't be wrong."

Taran turned slightly. "Stay quiet, Magh," he said gently. "Let me handle this."

He walked to the whiteboard, calm and deliberate. He listened to Rubesh's concerns, listing them on the left side of the board. On the right, he laid out the solution approach -

how the approach worked, how the industry interpreted it, and why it mattered.

Two hours passed. Taran didn't flinch. He balanced patience with precision, experience with empathy. By the end, Rubesh nodded. The sign-off was done.

As they left the room, Magh's hands were still shaking. She realized she'd jumped to defend herself too quickly - without building trust, without laying the groundwork.

Taran glanced at her. "Coffee?" he asked.

They walked in silence for five minutes before he spoke again. "I get it, Magh. You're new to people management. You'll learn. Just take down your key takeaways from today and apply them next time. Build your own work ethic from these moments. You'll get the hang of it."

He paused at the elevator. "Let's circle back on Rubesh's feedback tomorrow. And don't overthink it. Goodbye."

With that, he left the office.

Magh lingered, packing her bag slowly, her mind replaying every moment. Thirty minutes later, she stepped out - quiet, thoughtful, and just a little more prepared for the maze ahead.

It had been a heavy day.

As Magh walked home under the dim streetlights, her mind replayed every moment - the tension in the meeting room, the stumble with the projector, the way her voice had almost cracked. But more than anything, she carried a quiet resolve.

She knew she had work to do - not just on her reports or decks, but on herself. She wanted to build her own work ethic, one rooted in critical thinking, calm presence, and the ability to meet the expectations of her manager, her client, and her peers.

That evening, she opened her gratitude journal and wrote down her takeaway from the day while traveling back in the metro:

"I will learn to respond, not react. I will make my arguments stronger, not louder."

And like a child learning a new lesson, she wrote it ten times - each line a quiet promise to herself.

Her promise was not to be perfect, but to be better.

Two hours later, Magh arrived at the dinner her extended family had gathered for. Her sister Ichha had planned it all - to celebrate Magh's one-year milestone at work.

The moment she saw the cake, the words hit her like a quiet jolt: "Conquer the world."

Magh paused, her mind still tangled in the day's chaos. But as she stepped forward to cut the cake, she felt a wave of warmth. She turned and hugged Ichha tightly.

Ichha had a quiet elegance that turned heads without trying. Her short, curly hair - softly highlighted in warm brown tones - framed her wheatish complexion with effortless grace. She carried herself with a natural poise, her head always held high - not out of pride, but from experience of life. That night, she wore a satin black dress with playful polka dots - the same one she and Magh had picked out together weeks ago, laughing over patterns and colors like they always did.

Ichha had recently begun her PhD while also serving as a director at an NGO focused on early childhood care. She was the kind of woman who balanced intellect with empathy, ambition with grace.

The hug lingered, and Ichha could feel it - Magh was overwhelmed.

"We'll talk at home," Ichha whispered, her voice calm and grounding. "Live in the moment. This is your time to celebrate. I know you'll find your way through the work chaos - with patience and your own rhythm."

Magh smiled, pulling her into a side hug once more. Then she helped herself to a generous slice of chocolate cake and began greeting the rest of her family.

For the first time that day, she felt the weight lift - just a little.

"How's the new job treating you, Magh? How does it feel to be a corporate slave?" one of her aunts teased, a former sales executive with just enough edge in her voice to blur the line between joke and warning.

Everyone chuckled.

But the words 'corporate slave' clung to Magh's mind longer than the laughter did.

She paused, then replied - calm but certain.

"I'm just trying to figure out my own path. It's messy, sure - lots of twists and wrong turns. But at least it's mine, you know?"

She looked around, her voice steady but honest.

"It's too early to say much," Magh said, stirring her drink slowly. "But from the stories I hear from my managers… I've realized something. The ones who feel trapped - they've already given up. Corporate slavery isn't just a system. It's a mindset. If those same people shifted their lens, tried to shape chaos into opportunity… maybe they'd stop seeing chains and start seeing choices."

Her aunt gave a soft, knowing smile. "Easier said than done. But it's comforting to see the new generation trying to turn the tide."

Three hours later, the dinner chatter was just a memory. The drive home was quiet, save for the hum of the highway and the occasional flicker of streetlights.

That night, in her lilac pajamas - the ones with the little panda on the back, her spirit animal of lazy strength - Magh lay awake. The city lights blinked outside her window like coded messages she hadn't yet learned to read.

Would she be another sheep in the herd?

Or would she dare to tweak the script of a 9-to-infinity job?

She didn't have the answer.

But maybe, just maybe - the next day would bring her closer to it.

She closed her eyes and dreamt about it.

P.S. The corporate world doesn't come with a manual. It comes with moments - some that shake you, some that shape you. If you've ever felt stuck, questioned your path, or wondered if there's more to the maze than just survival... you're not alone. The journey ahead isn't about escaping the system. It's about rewriting your place within it. One choice, one mindset shift, one quiet promise at a time.

CHAPTER 3

TIME, TASKS & TRUTHS

"Mom, I'll be staying late in the office tonight," Saranya's voice echoed from the powder room - firm, focused, and not open for negotiation.

At her desk nearby, Sia slipped on her second glove, preparing to dive back into her work. Fair-skinned, tall, and strikingly lean, Sia had a presence that turned heads without trying. Her long, jet-black hair flowed down her back like a curtain - always perfectly brushed, always in place. She and Magh had joined the company together straight out of college, and though their personalities were different, their bond had stayed intact.

She leaned toward Magh and whispered with a mischievous grin, "Do you think there are sleeping pods in this office? Like back in college?"

Magh raised an eyebrow, barely looking up from her screen. "Let's tittle-tattle in the cab," she muttered. "I've got to send this deliverable by 7 p.m."

Sia rolled her eyes playfully and sank into her chair, the glow of her screen lighting up her face as the grind resumed.

It was the coldest day of the season. While leaving the office, Sia saw Saranya picking up a big cup of hot coffee to survive her night. As soon as she heard the story of the powder room, Magh said "Maybe she made a mistake at work today; our deliverables are way too complex, and this may be the reason she is probably staying in to rectify it."

Sia raised her brows and boarded her cab, slightly hinting at her discomfort with accepting the explanation.

Two days later, they both were late leaving the office as they missed their usual office cab. Three more taxis had been cancelled due to dense smog, which is usual for New Delhi. While juggling among taxi apps, they saw Saranya at the same coffee kiosk buying another big cup of coffee.

Sia anxiously questioned Magh, "Do you think she made another mistake or is it going to be like this for us too? Will the reality of what we heard from our seniors about the zero-work-life balance will hit us soon? Is she paid extra to clock more hours on her timesheet? I think it's high time I went and talk to her."

Being a fiery Aquarius, Sia didn't hold back. She walked briskly toward Saranya and asked, "Hey, do you live nearby? I've noticed you stay late most days."

Saranya looked up, unfazed. "Hi, dude. Not really. I've got deliverables pending, and traveling takes me two hours. I can't afford that kind of time loss right now."

Sia tilted her head. "Do you actually like doing overtime? Can't it wait till tomorrow? Or maybe ask for an extension? Does logging extra hours help with your appraisal?"

Saranya smirked. "Nobody forces me to overwork, and it doesn't boost my appraisal either. I do it when it's genuinely needed. I've been with the firm for years. Some days, the project runs so smoothly that I barely work eight hours. I even take two-hour lunch breaks when I can."

Sia nodded thoughtfully. "Fair enough. But I don't think I can stay late - even if the work demands it."

Saranya took a slow sip of her coffee and replied, "I've been here eight years. The one thing I've learned is this - I'll work hard, but not at the cost of my mental peace. I love what I do, so I'll show up early or stay late when it's really required. But I draw my own boundaries. If ending my day early helps me show up sharper tomorrow, I'll take that call."

Sia smiled. "Thanks for the chat. It was great hearing your perspective. My cab's almost here - I'll catch up with you tomorrow. I really want to learn how to be a happy and successful employee from leaders like you."

She waved goodbye and walked out, her long hair swaying behind her, thoughts swirling as fast as the city lights outside.

Meanwhile, Magh finished up her 2 emails and waited for Sia in the cab. The taxi driver ignited the engine and picked up Sia from the door next to the parking lot.

For the next twenty minutes, Magh was locked in a call with Rubesh, her voice steady but strained as she explained the delay in deliverables caused by an unforeseen issue. Sia, seated beside her, could only hear fragments - mostly Rubesh's sharp tone probing and pressing, each word landing like a blow.

Just then, Sia's phone buzzed. A message from Rubesh: "Need the deck by EOD."

Her heart sank. She had committed to delivering it in two days. No explanation, no context - just a deadline that had suddenly moved.

The cab rolled forward through the evening traffic, but inside, the silence was louder than the honks outside. Magh stared out the window, her phone still in hand. Sia sat stiffly, her mind racing through slides and timelines.

Neither spoke.

But the tension between them was palpable - an unspoken anxiety that hung in the air like static. Deadlines, expectations, pressure. It was just another day in the maze.

"This is infuriating,", said Sia, clenching her teeth, her cheeks turning red.

"Are you alright?", Magh gently asked.

"Why can't we stick to the agreed timeline? Why does Rubesh change at the last minute? I am a human, not a robot! I have a life at home too," Sia rolled her eyes and gazed outside with a deep sigh.

A few seconds later, Sia regained her composure and said, "I don't think I am cut out for a corporate job. I should think of joining my dad's business.".

Magh chose not to respond and looked away. She was in the midst of processing her last call where Rubesh briefly mentioned his intentions of escalating the issue.

The screech of the brakes caused a sudden jolt.

Magh swiftly reacted and asked Sia to take some deep breaths.

In a matter of seconds, Magh's composure cracked.

"I'm feeling anxious," she muttered, clutching her phone. "What if Rubesh escalates the project delay?"

Sia turned to respond, but before she could say a word, the cab driver glanced at them through the rearview mirror and smiled.

"Madam, sorry to jump into your conversation," he said gently. "My son works in a call center. I always tell him - I may not understand exactly what he does, but unless we're saving lives, we shouldn't let stress take over. We give our best, as long as we can. That's enough."

Magh blinked, caught off guard by the unexpected comfort.

The cab rolled on, but the tension had softened - just a little. Sometimes, wisdom comes from the most ordinary places.

His simple words had made their day.

Magh spent the rest of the cab ride with a soft smile on her face, the tension slowly melting away. Sia was dropped off at the temple she visited every evening with her mom - a ritual that grounded her, no matter how chaotic the day had been.

Later that night, at 11 p.m., Magh was about to set her alarm for 7 a.m. when her phone buzzed again. A new email arrived. She opened her Outlook app, and as the subject line loaded, a tear slipped quietly down her cheek.

It was her first client escalation.

She placed the phone aside, stood up, and paced slowly around her room. The walls felt closer than usual. She tapped play on her favorite instrumental playlist - the one that always helped her breathe a little easier.

Staring out the window, she whispered to herself, "College days were simpler. Fewer worries. I wish I could go back."

Then she remembered her dad's words: Never give up.

"I'll handle this," she said softly. "With patience. With a firm spirit. Nothing is beyond my reach."

She opened her laptop, took a deep breath, and began typing. Her response was clear and professional - addressing the concerns, explaining the delay, and assuring timely completion.

A few minutes later, she curled up in bed, the city lights blinking outside like quiet reminders.

And with that, she drifted off to sleep.

At 7AM, the sharp sound of the hummingbird bell echoed through the room. The screen lit up with "Rubesh calling".

To her surprise, it was not in her dreams. Magh picked up the phone immediately.

Rubesh inquired derogatorily, "Is the deliverable ready?"

She took a deep breath, sipped some water, and replied, "Hi Rubesh, Good morning. I hope you had a good sleep. I need another day to complete this with my team to give you better results. We are in the final stage of refining the deliverables and will be able to share by tomorrow."

He took a few seconds and responded. "I don't understand why you commit to something that you can't deliver on time. I can't allow any delay in the project. I want the deliverable today, by any means necessary," he yelled, clearly agitated.

After a deep breath, she finally spoke.

"I hear you Rubesh, I apologize for this delay. Let me sync up with my team and get back to you at the earliest."

Magh quickly dialed Taran, her fingers trembling slightly as the call connected. As soon as he picked up, she launched into the details - her voice quivering, but her words clear. She explained the call with Rubesh, the escalation, the delay. Panic hovered at the edge of her tone, but she held herself steady, determined to focus on the next steps.

On the other end, Taran listened without interruption.

"Take a deep breath, Magh," he said, his voice calm and even. "Have a sip of water. These things happen every day in our line of work. What matters is how we respond."

His words didn't erase the stress - but they anchored her, just enough to breathe again.

"Come to the office and let's work on the action plan. We will try to do our best. I will speak to Rubesh about what can be delivered by today. If a piece of work is delayed by 1 day, I am sure it will not change the world," he exclaimed. His tone was firm, shaped by years of experience.

Magh left her breakfast untouched, ignoring her mum's calls from the kitchen to wait while she packed some food. She didn't have the patience - not today. She grabbed her keys, ignited the engine, and drove herself to the office, skipping the usual wait for the company cab.

As she passed the junction where she sometimes picked up Sia, she remembered to inform her. She quickly typed out a message: "Will meet you directly at the office. God help me through the day."

It was short. Cryptic. But Sia understood immediately.

Something had gone wrong.

The tone, the timing, the plea - it all pointed to one thing: Magh's client had escalated the issue.

And the day had only just begun.

It was the first thing Sia had stumbled upon after a night spent hugging her 2-year-old dog Rookie. A golden longhair with a long body and short legs snuggled his head in Sia's elbow as she tried to climb out of the bed, as if he didn't want her to go to work leaving him behind.

She lifted him and put him down to play. In those few minutes of snuggles, she decided to call in sick at work. She immediately replied to Magh, "You got this girl. I know your client is tough, but I am assured that you will manage. Don't overthink and overwork yourself just like usual. I am not feeling too well this morning. I will be applying for sick leave today, see you tomorrow at work."

"Mom, let's take Rookie for a long walk today. I've called in sick at work," she shouted from the bedroom.

Her mom quickly ran towards her room, making a quick hair-bun of her long black hair.

"Are you alright Sia? What happened?" Meera asked out of concern.

"Nothing serious, Mom," Sia said, settling into the couch. "It's just… I've been working nonstop for over a year, and I've never taken a day off. The pressure's been building, and I'm learning it's okay to slow down sometimes. I sent the deliverable yesterday, and the client accepted it. So today, I just want to be with you and Rookie. After all the venting you've heard from me lately - I think I need to give you this time."

Meera smiled, brushing Sia's hair gently off her face. "I'm proud of you for saying that. You know, after teaching for twenty years, I've learned that every job is hard in its own way. But what matters most is how you treat yourself through it."

She paused, her voice soft but steady.

"You don't need to push yourself to the edge to prove anything. Taking a day to rest, to breathe, to be with family - that's not weakness. That's wisdom. And hearing you say this… it tells me you're not getting lost in the rush. You're trying to find your own way. That's the kind of strength that lasts."

Sia leaned into her mother's shoulder, comforted by the quiet truth in her words.

With a smile on her face and Rookie in her hands, Sia walked towards the door. She picked her workout water bottle and left for a long walk with her mom.

Meanwhile, Magh rushed towards the 5th floor as soon as she stepped out of the cab, breathing heavily.

Her voice vibrated with emotions as she greeted the team members she met on her way to the floor.

"Is everything ok with you?" the cleaner asked with a warm smile, as she greeted her every day.

Without a second glance, Magh began setting up her laptop, tuning out the voices around her. The mantras and life mottos shared by the cab driver the day before - though kind - did little to calm her nerves this morning.

She opened the Excel sheet and started walking Taran through the numbers as soon as he arrived. He listened patiently, then smiled and gestured toward the Nespresso machine just ten steps away.

"Come on," he said, offering a warm smile. "Let's grab a quick coffee."

To her surprise, he didn't mention the escalation - not a word - until she had finished her drink.

Then, with a light chuckle, he said, "I don't want another escalation regarding the quality of the deliverables. Your anxiety can seep into the work. Take a quick break when you need to - it's the only way to last long in any job. Otherwise, it'll eat you up."

Magh nodded, the warmth of the coffee grounding her more than the caffeine ever could.

Nine hours later, Magh finally clicked "Send." The sound of her sigh echoed across the quiet office floor - it was 9 p.m., and only a few lights still flickered overhead.

She and her two teammates stood up, stretched, and walked over to Taran's desk.

"Thanks for keeping us sane today," one of them said.

"Seriously," Magh added. "You didn't just guide us - you kept us calm."

Taran smiled, gave a small nod, and waved them off. "Grab a drink and take a break. You've carned it."

At the cab pickup point, the three of them sipped hot tea from paper cups, the steam rising into the cool night air. No one complained about the long hours. Not tonight.

One teammate chuckled, "You know, I always heard horror stories about managers in corporate firms. But today felt like a small win."

Magh smiled, her eyes soft. "Sometimes, it's just a mix of luck, a good attitude, and the right manager. That can change everything."

Just then, her phone lit up - Sia calling.

She picked up quickly. "Hey! I was just about to call you. I saw your texts but couldn't reply. It's been a crazy day. How is your health?"

Sia's voice was tired but firm. "I am feeling better. Are you okay?"

Magh exhaled. "Honestly? I was on the edge. I felt like I was falling apart. But somehow, I pulled through. Taran helped me see how I panic too fast, how I don't give myself space to think. That one coffee break with him changed my whole day. I wish more managers were like him - bold, clear, and uplifting."

There was a pause.

"It's almost 10 p.m. Are you still at the office?" Sia snapped, her voice sharp.

Magh hesitated. "Just leaving."

Sia didn't hold back. "I'm glad you're trying to stay positive. But this won't work if you keep burning yourself out. I don't want you to become like others - always exhausted, always chasing something that never pays back. These extra hours won't change your bank balance. Just remember - there are no free lunches. The choice is yours."

Magh didn't respond right away. She looked out at the quiet street, the tea cooling in her hand.

For the first time in her life, Magh was speechless. The silence on the call stretched longer than either of them expected - heavy, uncertain, and full of things unsaid. After a long pause, she finally whispered, "Goodnight."

She ended the call.

But the words didn't end there. They lingered, circling her thoughts as she lay in bed. And even as sleep gently pulled her under, they followed - soft, persistent, and unresolved.

P.S. Magh thought she had survived the storm. But what if the real challenge wasn't the escalation, or the deliverable - but learning how to protect her peace in a world that rarely pauses? Tomorrow would bring new emails, new expectations, and maybe... a new decision.

CHAPTER 4

WHEN PLANS CHANGE

"I am resigning today," Sia said firmly, starting another busy day at work.

"After three years of navigating endless twists and turns, I'm done. This is not my cup of tea. I want to build something of my own."

She paused, then looked at Magh with a soft smile.

"You've been the best part of this place. Not just a coworker - my friend for life."

Magh spun her chair around with a sudden jerk, her face flushing pale and red. She stared at Sia, stunned.

"Wait - what? This isn't a joke, right? Have you really thought this through?" she asked, her voice trembling.

Sia gave a gentle smile. "I'm sorry to drop this on your birthday, but it's not the first time I've considered it. Every escalation, every impossible deadline... they've made me question if this is what I want to do for the rest of my life."

She paused, her eyes steady.

"There are still pieces missing in my plan, but the peace I feel knowing I'm choosing what's right for my mental well-being - that's priceless. I'll figure out the rest. Maybe I'll fail, maybe I'll come back. But today, this feels right."

Magh exhaled slowly, her shoulders sinking.

"I wasn't expecting this kind of surprise today," she said quietly. "But I'm happy for you. You'll be out of this grind soon. I'll miss you around here… a lot."

Sia reached out and squeezed her hand.

"I'll miss you too," Sia said, her voice warm but resolute. "But this isn't goodbye - it's just the start of something new. We'll stay in touch, of course."

She paused, looking at Magh with quiet sincerity.

"I don't know if you truly enjoy what you're doing. Maybe you don't have the answer yet. But remember what that cab driver said the other day - we're all just puppets in this corporate maze. Find your own path, Magh. Don't lose yourself in it."

Her words lingered, not as advice, but as a gentle nudge toward something deeper - something Magh hadn't dared to ask herself in a long time.

Before Magh could respond to Sia's parting words, a message popped up in the WhatsApp workgroup.

Taran: "Pantry, 5 mins. Birthday celebration for Magh!"

She blinked at the screen. It was her third year in the corporate world - and the first time she hadn't taken the day off on her birthday. This one felt different: no carefree brunches, no long calls with college friends, just deadlines, escalations, and a quiet ache she couldn't quite name.

As she walked toward the pantry, flashes of past birthdays danced through her mind - laughter, cake fights, spontaneous road trips. For a moment, she wanted to turn around, skip the candles, and disappear into her desk.

But then she saw it.

A rich chocolate cake, perfectly frosted, with a tag that read: "Happy Birthday, Consultant."

She froze.

In that quiet moment, as her colleagues gathered and began singing, Magh stood still - watching, listening, but somewhere else entirely. The word Consultant stared back at her, not just as a title, but as a reminder of how far she'd come... and how far she still had to go.

One thought echoed in her mind, clear and unwavering: Change is the only constant.

Her smile was faint, but real. And while the others clapped and cheered, she made a silent promise to herself - to embrace the change, whatever it looked like.

Sia handed her resignation letter to HR with a quiet smile, the weight she'd been carrying finally lifting off her shoulders. A few minutes later, she slipped into the pantry just as the birthday celebration was winding down - half-eaten cake, soft laughter, and the hum of tired voices.

She spotted Magh near the counter and walked straight to her, wrapping her arms around her in a tight hug.

"Happy birthday," she whispered, holding on for a moment longer than usual.

Magh pulled back, surprised. "Are you okay?"

Sia leaned in, her voice low but steady. "I feel free today, Magh. I finally did it - I quit."

Magh's eyes widened. "You actually went through with it?"

Sia nodded. "Yeah. It's not about giving up. I just… I want to follow what's been tugging at me for so long. I know corporate life will be the same wherever I go, but this - this is my choice. My path. If I don't take the leap now, I'll never get closer to the life I dream of."

Magh looked at her, speechless for a moment, then smiled softly. "You're brave, Sia. I'm proud of you. I just wish I had that kind of clarity. I do enjoy what I'm doing, and I could probably keep going for years… but the pressure from difficult clients and demanding managers - it wears me down. Sometimes I think about quitting too. But then I remember the home loan, the lack of time to even look for something else, and the fear that every other job might feel the same. That's what keeps me here."

Sia took a slow sip of water, then leaned in gently. "Set your goals and wants clearly, Magh. Once you do, you'll find time for them. Whether it's switching jobs or rethinking your career entirely, clarity helps everything fall into place. A month ago, I couldn't have imagined handing in my resignation. My head was full of doubts. But the one thing I held onto was this - choosing my mental health over my paycheck. I read somewhere that when your mind is at peace, making money might take longer… but it's never impossible."

Magh's voice trembled as she replied, "I hear you. The way you look at life - it feels like a gift. And on my birthday, no less. I don't know if I'll ever be able to fully unwrap it, but I'll start… slowly. For the sake of both my health and my career. And yes, I'll work on prioritizing my peace too."

Sia smiled and pulled her into a side hug, quiet confidence in her eyes.

Together, they picked up a generous slice of cake and walked back toward their desks - two friends, side by side, each carrying a different kind of hope.

Three months later, the team gathered to bid farewell to Sia. She left with a smile and a quiet sense of purpose, ready to chase the path she had chosen for herself.

Meanwhile, Magh transitioned into a new project under Rubesh's extended team, with Taran offering part-time supervision. On paper, it looked familiar - names she knew, systems she'd seen - but the reality felt worlds apart from the comfort she'd built over the last three years.

Though familiar faces led the way, everything else was new. The people, the culture, the pace, even the technology - it all demanded a fresh start.

Each day felt like rebuilding from the ground up. And while Taran's presence offered a sense of continuity, the dynamics around her shifted constantly, leaving her to navigate unfamiliar expectations and mentally taxing challenges.

The first few months were a blur of meetings, briefing calls, and silent observations. It wasn't the physical effort that wore her down - it was the mental weight: the constant need to adapt, to prove herself, to stay afloat in a sea of shifting dynamics. Most evenings, she returned home drained, her thoughts tangled in unfinished tasks and unread emails.

Each day felt like a relentless battle. One moment, Magh was scrambling to meet the sky-high expectations of a demanding client; the next, she was swallowing the sting of casual disrespect that left her simmering. It became a pattern - her efforts overlooked, her frustrations brushed aside.

The quiet storm inside her grew louder.

She showed up, she delivered, she tried. But recognition never came. And with every passing day, the mental toll deepened - not from the work itself, but from the constant fight to be seen, heard, and valued.

Most of her work friends were all in the same boat, each of them trapped in the never-ending cycle of long, gruelling days that bled into late-night team dinners and the exhausting two-hour journey back home. The routine was draining, predictable, suffocating, and leaving no space for anything beyond the demands of work. She felt herself slowly losing her sense of self, caught in a web of expectations and responsibilities.

In a desperate attempt to break free, she decided to join a gym near her client's office. She had to find something - anything that would allow her to breathe. By the time she returned home after her long days, she was completely drained, both physically and emotionally, and there was no energy left for herself.

So, she began waking up at 6 a.m. every morning, stepping out into the harsh cold of Delhi's winter, her body protesting with each step, but her mind pushing her forward. It wasn't easy. But somehow, despite the exhaustion that weighed her down, she was hitting the gym at 8 a.m. sharp every single day for nearly two months, before diving straight into another relentless work shift.

She wasn't just fighting for fitness; she was fighting for a piece of herself. A small, sacred moment where she could feel alive, where the chaos of her life didn't have the final say. And though it was hard, she held on to that quiet hope, maybe this small change would make a difference.

Six months had passed, and she felt like a programmed robot, moving through her days on autopilot, struggling to keep her mind at peace. The exhaustion was no longer just physical; it had seeped into her soul. As a Leo, she prided herself on her strength, her fierce determination to push through any obstacle. She tried hitting every wall - working harder, convincing herself it was just a phase, that she could handle it. But each day felt more like a battle, and slowly, the weight of it all started to crush her spirit.

Finally, she reached a breaking point. She couldn't keep pretending everything was fine when it wasn't. She realized, with a sharp clarity, that she couldn't survive working with Rubesh and team any longer. It wasn't just the work - it was the constant pressure, the disrespect, the toll it was taking on her mental and emotional well-being. It was no longer her fight to win, nor her cup of tea to sip. And as much as it pained her to admit it, she knew it was time to walk away.

Over the next two months, Magh stuck to a quiet promise she made to herself - fifteen minutes a day, dedicated solely to applying for new jobs. It wasn't much, but it was something. A small act of hope in the middle of long, draining workdays.

She faced rejections. She faced interviewers who dissected every technical detail she had ever learned, leaving her second-guessing her own skills. And with each passing day, the mental exhaustion from her current role made it harder to stay motivated. The fear of not finding something better loomed large.

One question kept surfacing in interviews, and it always made her pause: *"Why do you want to switch so early in your career?"*

She never had a clear answer. Not one she could articulate without sounding unsure. After a few interviews, she realized her feelings about switching jobs were tangled - hopeful one day, hesitant the next. Some mornings, she believed a new place could offer something better. Other days, she simply craved change. A shift in the 3Ps: People, Paycheck, and Problems.

She couldn't yet describe what she was looking for. But she knew what she wanted to leave behind. And sometimes, that was enough to keep going.

After two months of juggling her demanding job and countless rounds of interviews, Magh finally made it.

On the eve of her favorite festival - Christmas - she received a gift she hadn't dared to expect: an offer letter from a new company, a bank, offering her a role aligned with her interests. It felt like Santa had heard her silent prayers.

Just after lighting candles at her nearby church with Ichha, she opened the email. The subject line alone made her heart race. As she scrolled through the offer letter, her eyes welled up. She hadn't imagined this moment would feel so overwhelming.

In an instant, memories came rushing back - the first day she walked into the ARC office, nervous but hopeful; the little dance she did in the powder room when she landed her first client project; the late nights, the quiet wins, the friendships, the frustrations. It all played like a reel in her mind.

This wasn't just a job offer. It was a turning point. A quiet affirmation that her persistence, her resilience, and her belief in something better had finally paid off.

Lost in a swirl of memories, Magh barely noticed the gentle nudge from Ichha beside her.

"It's time to look ahead," Ichha said softly. "I know change can feel unsettling, but it's the one thing we can count on. The new company might still have its own grind, its own version of corporate chaos - but this shift isn't just about work. It's about growth. It's about choosing something better for yourself."

Magh turned to her, eyes misty.

"And it's not just you," Ichha continued. "We're in this together. This step forward - it brings us closer to the life we've been dreaming of: the home we've been building piece by piece, and relief from the weight of those loans that never seem to loosen their grip. That promised increment? It might be the first real breath of relief we've had in years."

She paused, her voice steady but full of emotion.

"It's not just about the paycheck. It's about every late night, every compromise, every moment we told ourselves to hold on a little longer. We're closer now than ever before."

Magh offered a warm smile, though it trembled with a mix of excitement and uncertainty. Her fingers hovered over the trackpad, hesitating for just a moment before clicking "Send."

The signed contract was gone - her decision sealed.

It wasn't just a new job. It was the end of a chapter she had lived and breathed for so long. The weight of change pressed against her chest, but the promise of growth, of new beginnings, pulled her forward.

Even if it meant sailing into unknown waters, she was ready to move. Not just for herself - but for the life she was building, one step at a time.

Two days later, after Christmas break, she walked into the client's office. A deep sigh escaped her lips as she pushed through the door. She gave herself a break - not just from the gym, but from the constant pressure to keep everything in motion. She allowed herself a moment to breathe, to simply be present.

Dropping her bag at her desk, she made her way to the nearby phone booth. She called Taran to share the news of her resignation. After a brief silence, he suggested they meet in person the next day before he could formally accept the resignation. The weight of the conversation hung in the air, but for the first time in a long while, she felt a strange relief, like she was finally taking control of her own path.

Throughout the day, she kept her focus sharp and her commitment to her work. Like a true professional, she gave no hints to anyone around her about the decision she had already made.

The next morning, she arrived at the office at 9 a.m. sharp, still carrying the calm energy from her workout.

As they settled into the pantry, steaming cups of masala chai in hand, Magh knew the moment had come. With a steady breath, she spoke the words that had been weighing on her heart.

"I have decided to resign today. Thank you for the learning opportunities with you and your team," Magh said, her voice calm yet resolute.

Taran listened carefully, his gaze steady and composed. After a thoughtful pause, he said, "I accept your resignation, Magh. But the final decision will rest with Navneet. He will need to find your replacement quickly - this shouldn't impact our project deliverables. Please inform him and ensure the timeline stays intact."

Magh nodded, her heart heavy, "Thank you, Taran. I'll take it forward with the team."

Back at her desk, she drafted the email with quiet precision - addressed to Navneet and his assistant, with Taran marked in CC for transparency, though he was on personal leave for the next two weeks. She read it twice before hitting send, her fingers lingering on the keyboard.

Then came silence.

Two days passed, and the thread remained untouched. No reply, no acknowledgement.

On the third day, after the morning stand-up, something shifted in her. She couldn't carry the weight of uncertainty any longer. That evening, she left her client's office early, her mind set. She needed to be in the ARC office - not just to follow up, but to reclaim her voice.

After a cab canceled on her, she hopped into an auto that happened to pass by, making sure to reach before 6 p.m. sharp - the official closing time, at least on paper. She rushed up in the elevator, breathless, and made her way to the fifth floor. As she glanced through the glass door of Navneet's cabin, she saw him on the phone. She quickly found a nearby desk, pulled out her laptop, and connected to the internet to check his next availability on Microsoft Teams.

The moment his status switched to "Available", she knocked on the door. With her laptop in her left hand, she waited for his acknowledgment. He looked up, smiled, and gestured for her to come in. She opened the door, stepped inside, and placed her laptop on one side of the desk before taking the seat he offered. She knew this would be a difficult conversation, but her decision was firm.

With a few seconds of eye contact passed and the unforgettable words uttered, "I am not accepting your resignation, Magh, you have a lot to learn and contribute to the team. You are one of the key assets to this firm. You have so much more to learn, so much more to contribute," he continued, his tone firm but not unkind. "You're one of the key assets to this firm. All three of you - hired straight from campus - are full of energy, full of ideas. I chose each of you for a reason. I've gone back to your college every year to build a team that could lead, not just follow. A team where you all will become leaders in the future to run projects on your own and not give up and settle for a slow-paced job to find work-life balance."

It wasn't a surprise to Magh - but it was overwhelming. In that moment, she felt the full weight of the stature she had quietly built over the past three years. The recognition, the trust, the belief others had in her - it all came rushing in, not as praise, but as a reflection of the journey she had walked, often unnoticed, often doubted, yet undeniably impactful.

She smiled, her heart fluttering at the praise, and responded, "Thanks, Navneet, it means a lot coming from you, but I have thought through this decision for my career and the move that will help me fulfill more of my family responsibilities."

"You have your entire life to live for your family. I have no say in that. The opportunities I have planned for all campus hires in the team will take you a long way in your career. If you say you have thought through this decision, can you tell me where you are joining next, what your role will be there, and how it will differentiate you from your current work identity that you have built with us ?", he questioned, his voice steady and firm.

There was a long silence, the kind that stretched on just a little too long, making her feel uneasy. She fidgeted with the hem of her sleeve, her mind racing. She knew the answers partially - she had done her research, asked around, and had a sense of what the new role entailed-but doubt lingered. Was she truly ready? She wasn't entirely sure if she had the clarity to make the switch.

"I am joining the firm where you worked previously," she began, her voice trembling slightly as she spoke. "The role is similar to what I did for our last banking client. I may not be entirely clear about the day-to-day responsibilities at the PKC Bank in depth, but I believe I'll gain the work-life balance that will help me maintain a relaxed mind. Plus, the salary is better," Magh said, her voice soft but steady. "It's not just about the numbers - it's about what those numbers mean. You know I've been carrying the weight of my home loan, month after month. This offer gives me a little breathing room. A chance to support my family without constantly worrying if I'm falling behind. It's not just a job change - it's a step toward stability, toward something I've been working so hard to build."

She paused for a moment, her eyes avoiding Navneet's gaze as she tried to steady herself.

Navneet smirked, a low chuckle escaping his lips. "That's great to hear," he said, his tone tinged with sarcasm. "Maybe you'll be happy and 'relaxed' there."

He leaned back slightly, eyes narrowing with a mix of amusement and challenge.

"But tell me, Magh - do you really want that? You've only just begun your career. Is this the time to settle into a backseat role? One where the work becomes routine, the pace slows down, and the challenges fade into seasonal bursts of chaos? Especially now, when you're still shaping your foundation?"

He leaned back in his chair, folding his arms. "You're so young, full of potential. You should be chasing fast-paced, high-stakes opportunities - not settling for something that'll make you feel retired before you've even truly begun."

She took a deep breath, steadying herself before speaking, her voice low but unwavering.

"I hear you, and I truly respect your perspective. But for me, it's not just about the work or the role on paper. It's everything around it. I've been feeling overwhelmed at the client site - like I'm constantly running on empty. I try to bring ideas to the table, to think creatively, but they're dismissed before they even land. You've seen how Rubesh treats consultants like us - it's hard to feel heard, let alone valued."

She paused, her eyes searching for a flicker of understanding.

"It's starting to feel like I'm failing… even though I'm giving it everything I've got. And that's a hard place to be in, day after day."

She paused, her voice a bit quieter now, as if she was weighing her words carefully. "I know it might sound like I'm seeking something easier, but it's not that. The truth is, the incremental raise at PKC, even though it may be a game changer, will actually help me more than the innovation I keep trying to push here. At this point, the financial security for my family feels like a bigger priority than continuing to fight for something that seems to get dismissed at every turn."

Navneet leaned forward slightly, his tone shifting to a more persuasive one. "If the client is your concern, we can work that out," he said. "I'm not blind to your potential, and I believe we can create a path where you feel more supported. In fact, I have a big pipeline coming up, and there are several onsite opportunities where you'll have the chance to learn and make more money at the same time," he said.

He paused, his smile almost sly, eyes narrowing with a hint of nostalgia.

"Isn't traveling one of your biggest personal goals?" he asked, his voice calm but deliberate. "I remember during your interview - you spoke with such excitement about wanting those experiences. The exposure, the learning, the thrill of new places."

He leaned forward slightly, his tone softening.

"You crave challenges, Magh. You've always wanted to grow, to stretch beyond the ordinary. This role - it might be the perfect way to do both. The discomfort you're feeling now… it's part of the process. Part of becoming who you're meant to be."

He let the words settle before adding, "I think it's worth reconsidering. Before you make a final decision, ask yourself - are you walking away from something hard, or toward something better?"

She looked her boss in the eye, taking a moment to gather her thoughts before speaking with a calm, steady voice. "I really appreciate that you've considered me for these opportunities, and I value the faith you have in me. My experience working at ARC is like building the spine of my career. However, at this moment, my mind is firm. I believe stepping into this new role at PKC Bank is the best choice for me and my future. I would like you to accept my resignation. This is not an easy decision, but I feel it's the right one for me right now."

His expression shifted to one of disappointment, though his tone remained calm and professional. "I can't force you to stay, and I've presented all the facts to give you a clear picture of your future with this firm. I respect your decision, but I'm still not convinced. You're making a choice based on what you feel now, and that's understandable, but I do want you to think it through. I'll email HR to formalize your resignation, but I'd ask you to keep re-evaluating your decision. Speak with other managers like Saranya and Taran who see your potential, talk to those who are already on site, living the experience, seeing the world with the corporate hustle, and making money by saving their per diem and supporting their families. The reality of this career can be different from what you're imagining. During your notice period, I'll wait for you to circle back on your thoughts. If, in the next three months, you change your mind, I'm here to listen."

She gave a small, appreciative smile, though her decision was unwavering. "It was a great discussion, as always. Thank you for your understanding and for giving me all the opportunities to grow here."

She stood up and picked up her laptop in her left hand. Turning toward him, she extended her hand for a firm handshake. "I thank you for every opportunity, Navneet. You are an incredible leader whom I am not sure I will ever find in any organization," she said, her voice calm yet determined.

With a final nod, she turned and walked out of his cabin, feeling the weight of her decision but confident in the path she had chosen.

As Magh stepped out of Navneet's cabin, her thoughts still tangled in the conversation they'd just had, her phone buzzed. She glanced down, expecting a routine notification - but froze when she saw it.

Outlook: "Resignation Acceptance."

Her heart skipped a beat.

It was from Navneet, addressed to HR. She tapped it open, her breath catching as she read the words. "I wish Magh the very best for her future. Please proceed with formalities and set her final working day three months from today."

She stood still, just a few paces from her desk, the weight of the moment pressing down on her. The decision she had wrestled with for weeks was now real - no longer a thought, no longer a draft in her inbox. It was official.

And yet, her mind was still reeling from Navneet's parting words: the praise, the challenge, and the subtle push to reconsider. But now, the door had been opened. The countdown had begun.

The countdown was for three months.

A swirl of emotions flooded her, but she composed herself, taking a deep breath before walking back to her desk. She packed her laptop into her bag, then grabbed her lunch box. She silently declared the day over. Skipping the office shuttle, she hailed a cab and headed straight home, her thoughts drifting as the city passed by outside the window.

The next morning she gave a call to her old friend Sia to share the resignation news as soon as she boarded her client office shuttle. "Hi Sia, How are you? I want to share some news with you that will make your day. I handed in my resignation yesterday. I am joining PKC Bank in the next three months," she spoke, with a voice full of excitement.

"Congratulations, Magh, I am happy to hear this. Did you talk to people working at the PKC Bank apart from interviewers? Will it be any different to what you are doing now? Sia questioned, her mind seemed to be perplexed.

"I haven't, she said. But I know about the team I will be working with. The increment is good and I am hoping to get a relaxed environment", she replied, with a strong, yet shaky voice.

Sia chuckled, "So a new race, new players but the same corporate chaos?"

A sudden long pause lingered in the air.

"It may be, maybe it will always be. I can't take risks like you Sia," she said. "I may switch the boats in the midst of this chaos, but I may not be completely out of the woods anytime soon. I like the recurring paychecks; I plan my life based on that. I take debts accordingly. If I drop out once, everything will fall apart. The growth may be challenging and slow, unlike big business returns, but it gives me strength to sleep peacefully at the end of the day, a relaxed mind for some hours, dreaming and waiting for the next paycheck."

"I understand, but maybe I can't fully relate at this point in time," she said, her voice soft yet firm.

"But I hear you. Starting a business isn't easy either. And it's certainly not a quick fix to escape corporate slavery. It has its own set of pros and cons. The grass always seems to be greener on the other side. I'm sure you'll handle the downsides of your job, and I'll figure out how to manage the challenges of the business world. At the end of the day, I think what we both need to learn is how to keep ourselves sane and happy. I truly wish you the best for this new role. Let's catch up over a drink soon," she concluded, her words resonating between them.

"I totally agree with you," Magh replied, her tone reflecting a shared understanding. "We have to find our happiness where we are. See you soon, Sia," she added, before ending the call.

Two hours later, after crossing heavy Delhi traffic, she reached her client's place. She alighted from the bus, walked through the glass door towards the lift. She entered the lift and bumped into Rubesh, one of the strong reasons she had decided to quit. Within a second, as the lift doors closed, ignoring the presence of others in the lift, Rubesh said, looking directly in her eyes with a strong rage, "Read the official email this morning about your resignation. Tell Taran to hire someone who can handle me more than work, I can do your job too but I am at a higher position now as you know."

He walked out of the lift on the next floor as the elevator opened. Magh could not respond to him and kept looking down at her phone, making no eye contact with others in the lift until she reached her floor.

As she stepped out of the lift, she went directly to the pantry and gulped a full glass of water. She took a deep breath, smiling and looking through the glass window in the pantry as if thanking her daylight stars for the decision she had made.

She walked to her workspace where she was welcomed with strange eyes, eyes full of questions from her team who were informed about her resignation. Deflecting the expressions, she greeted everyone and kept her laptop bag on the desk, took out her laptop, logged in, and started checking her emails.

An hour later, Rubesh came to her desk, no greeting today, just the usual brisk command. "Prepare a transition plan," he instructed, his tone clipped. "Make sure all current projects are completed before your last day."

It wasn't a surprise. The deadline was inevitable, but the weight of it still pressed on her chest. What had once been a six-month timeline had now been slashed to just three, and in addition to the regular workload, there was the daunting task of ensuring everything was handed over smoothly. It felt like a mountain to climb in half the time.

She exhaled slowly, knowing she'd have to summon every ounce of energy to this final task for her tyrannical manager.

For the next two months, she threw herself into her work with steadfast dedication, as if she were an employee who had no intention of leaving. Every task, every deadline was met with precision, driven by a sense of responsibility that pushed her to give her all. But beneath the surface of relentless professionalism, she also made a quiet promise to herself - she would reclaim the time lost. Even as the tasks piled up, she found moments to reconnect with her health and her family, balancing the demands of work with the needs of her well-being. It was a delicate dance, but one she was determined to master before her final day.

Though she had no clue what was coming next in her new job, one thing had become clear during her notice period. When you reach a point where you feel you have nothing left to lose, your approach to work changes. There's freedom in it. With nothing to prove, no fear of failure, her mind found a rare peace. She worked more efficiently, less encumbered by stress, and paradoxically, felt more in control. She couldn't quite balance everything perfectly, but she didn't fall every day trying to. It was a lesson she'd carry forward, knowing that sometimes, letting go was the key to moving forward.

During the last month of her notice period, Taran reached out to her. He called to ask if she'd be interested in catching up over coffee.

Being assertive was something she had always tried to master but had never fully achieved. Nevertheless, she scheduled a time for the following week. During their brief conversation, she mentioned that she was in the process of wrapping up her responsibilities and handing over her work to the new hire who would take over her role. She also informed him that she would be working from the ARC office for her final three weeks with the firm.

Taran agreed to wait and confirmed their coffee catch-up plan, leaving her to wonder what the meeting might bring.

Finally, she completed all the tasks assigned to her and successfully prepared the new hire to take over the reins and chase the deadlines ahead. To her surprise, someone from Rubesh's team had ordered a farewell cake to bid her adieu from the client site.

As the day came to an end, everyone gathered to say their goodbyes. She stood by the cake, cut it, and gave a brief, heartfelt speech. "Thank you, everyone, for helping me learn and grow. It's been a pleasure working with all of you, and I hope our paths cross again someday."

Rubesh and the team expressed their gratitude and wished her the best of luck in her future endeavors. One of her peers mentioned planning a grand farewell party on her official last day with ARC, three weeks from then. The group shared in the cake and laughter, but at precisely 6 p.m., Magh left, submitting her client vendor card at the reception, smiling, making sure to walk out without looking back.

As she made her way home, mixed thoughts swirled in her mind. The way people had greeted her on her last day had left her feeling special, proud of the work she had done. While her efforts hadn't always been respected during her project stints, the appreciation she received that day overwhelmed her. People aren't inherently bad, she reflected. Maybe it's the pressure of the corporate world, the expectations from leadership, that shapes how they behave in a certain way. She reassured herself, knowing that sometimes, circumstances dictate actions more than individual intentions.

After a relaxing weekend getaway with her family at the Neemrana Fort in Jaipur, celebrating her sister's 30th birthday, she returned to the office promptly at 9 a.m. It might sound odd to some readers that, even during her notice period, she adhered strictly to office hours. But for her, it wasn't just about the job. It was about the first paycheck she had ever received from this firm. That smile on her parents' faces when she shared the news was priceless. Her father had taken a screenshot of her salary credit message and placed it directly in the family temple, thanking God for the largest salary credit they'd ever seen for their family of four.

He couldn't help but chuckle as he remembered his own first earnings. He had placed that money in his mother's hands, and she, in turn, had kept it in the temple. Now, in this world of technology, the digital message of her salary credit had found its way into the temple instead. He smirked, amused by how much the world had changed. Her mom, standing beside her dad, wiped a tear from her eye, overwhelmed by the journey their family had made.

The memories faded like mist as the elevator dinged softly.

As soon as she reached the fifth floor, she spotted Taran sitting casually in the bay next to her workspace. He leaned back in his ergonomic chair, one leg crossed over the other, a relaxed posture that contrasted with the usual hustle of the office. His desk was neatly organized, with a few papers scattered beside his laptop, the soft hum of the office filling the air around him. She waved at him, and he smiled back, continuing his conversation on a Teams call. With a subtle gesture, he signalled to Magh that he would come over to speak with her shortly.

As she dropped her laptop bag onto the desk, she opened her inbox, her eyes scanning the screen mechanically, when she noticed him - Navneet. He passed by her desk, engaged in a conversation with Taran, but made no attempt to even glance in her direction. Not a brief acknowledgment, not a casual nod. Just... nothing. He walked back to his cabin without a second thought, his presence already fading into the backdrop of the office.

A cold feeling settled in her chest. The invisible weight of it pressed down, making her feel like she wasn't even there.

The memory of Sia's forwarded WhatsApp message surfaced suddenly, sharp and clear in her mind. "Everyone is replaceable in the corporate world. You step out of the corporate maze, and the next player is already ready to play the game." The words stung more than ever now, as she sat there, unseen and unnoticed, her place in the company fading with every passing moment.

An hour later, as she sat lost in the rhythm of her thoughts, Taran approached her desk with a smile that seemed more genuine than usual. "Are you serious about leaving us and joining PKC?" he asked, his tone a mix of disbelief and concern. "I don't think I can let this happen. You need a drink with me more than a cup of coffee," he added, chuckling softly.

Her mind went blank for a moment, as if time itself had frozen. The words hung in the air, but they didn't immediately register. She stared at him, not sure how to respond.

In that brief pause, her thoughts spiraled. Every employee has a different story, she mused, her mind drifting back to the countless faces she'd passed in the hallways, the projects she'd worked on, the late nights and early mornings. We may be replaceable but we can end our story with a long-lasting connection with the people we work with. Her chest tightened, the weight of Taran's words a mix of warmth and overwhelming pressure.

A warm smile curved at the corners of her lips, softening the weight of the conversation. She took a breath before replying, her tone steady, though there was a hint of something deeper lurking beneath. "I appreciate your thoughts, Taran," she began, her gaze meeting his, her eyes carrying a quiet resolve. "But I've thought this through. The offer from PKC is good - it's something that could help me grow, not just professionally, but in my personal life as well. It's a chance for me to make a real change, to step up in ways I've been hoping for. I've got 15 working days left, and I want to make sure I leave with everything wrapped up, all my responsibilities taken care of."

Taran's expression shifted slightly, his brow furrowing as his tone grew firmer. "I'm not convinced. Not by this, and certainly not by Navneet's silence," he said, his voice taking on an edge that was almost protective. "Look, I'm not saying this to pressure you, but I know the value of all you campus hires who have potential to grow with the opportunities and projects coming soon. Staying with a company for the long haul - seeing things through - helps you grow more than you think. There are so many projects we've been considering for you as well to involve you in so many other opportunities ahead. Our team is growing, and I suggest you reconsider."

For the next thirty minutes, Taran sat beside her, sharing his professional experience of the last 20 years. He highlighted the potential growth, the enticing prospects of onsite opportunities that could help her learn, save, and even achieve her travel goals.

Magh listened, but her mind was spinning. Her emotions were a tangled mess. She was too young to be making such life-altering decisions, wasn't she? She'd always thought of herself as someone who could juggle her goals, but now, with Taran laying out the facts, she felt like she was standing at a crossroads, unsure of which direction to take. The corporate maze of her new job loomed before her, an unknown world, and she had no idea how different or similar it would be to this one.

Her thoughts were a blur, caught between the balance of life, family, money, and passion. Her decision had seemed firm when she first made it, but now the reality of it was hitting harder than she'd anticipated. Her millennial confidence, the self-assurance she had always prided herself on, was now shaken. It felt like the foundation beneath her was slowly crumbling.

For as long as she could remember, whenever faced with tough choices, she had always sought her dad's advice. But this decision was different. Her dad wasn't just any man - he was an entrepreneur, a man who had built his own path without the steady security of a corporate job. She recalled the conversation they'd had when she first mentioned the new offer to him. His words echoed in her mind, quiet but powerful: "Whatever decision you make, Magh, make sure it's not impulsive and driven by money. Money is like dirt in your hands. You have it today, or you won't have it tomorrow."

Her father's wisdom weighed heavily on her as the minutes ticked by. She closed her eyes for a moment, gathering her swirling thoughts. It felt like an eternity before she found the words to respond, the weight of the conversation thick in the air between them.

"I don't know if the decision I made is the right one," she finally said, her voice barely above a whisper. "But I'm overwhelmed to see how much energy has gone into convincing me to stay, not just by the numbers and future plans, but by how all the seniors here are trying to help me see how this could shape my future. I can't deny that. I'm not sure if the experience you shared with me today or the long-term vision you laid out will change my decision, though."

Taran smiled softly, his expression genuine. "Take your time, Magh," he said, his voice warm, even though there was a hint of humor underneath. "You've got all the time in the world. Digest what I've explained to you informed by my experience. Let's talk again tomorrow, and we can discuss it further. I'm a consultant, after all," he added with a playful grin, his voice lightening the mood.

Magh nodded, grateful for the space he was giving her. She watched as Taran turned and walked back to his desk, his footsteps echoing in the quiet of the office. She let herself sit in the silence for a moment longer, the decision still hanging heavy, but the space to think, to breathe, was almost a relief.

And with that, she turned back to her work, the weight of the day still pressing on her shoulders, but for now, the next step would wait.

Two hours later, as Magh walked toward the powder room, her mind still tangled in the conversation with Taran, she crossed the elevator lobby and unexpectedly bumped into Navneet. She paused for a moment, feeling the familiar shakiness rush through her again. The sense of non-existence she had felt earlier in the day resurfaced, flooding her thoughts with a new wave of doubt. Her first instinct was to continue walking, to pretend as if everything was fine, to flash him a polite smile and move past him.

But to her surprise, Navneet didn't step into the elevator as expected. Instead, he turned toward her, his posture composed, his presence unwavering.

"Good to see you, Magh," he said, his tone clipped and businesslike. "So… when are you taking your resignation back?"

She blinked, caught off guard.

"I still haven't heard from you," he continued, "about how your role at PKC will be any different - aside from the salary bump."

His gaze held hers, steady and challenging.

"You know," he added, "if you join the upcoming project in Cape Town, the exposure, the savings - it'll be similar to what you're thinking of making at PKC. Especially with your next appraisal coming up. You're already on track."

Magh's heart skipped a beat. She stood there, frozen for a moment, letting his words hang in the air. She didn't respond immediately, her mind racing to catch up with the sudden shift in energy between them. She simply kept listening, feeling the weight of his words sink in, even as she struggled to find her voice.

Navneet didn't stop there. He continued, unbothered by her silence. "The current project team from Cape Town is returning today. You should speak to Saranya about the opportunities you could explore there. Weigh all your options, Magh. Not every organization offers the kind of chances we're giving you here, something you are so passionate about. I've already spoken to Saranya, and she'll talk to you. I'm keen to see how you assess this for your own benefit, just like when you made the right decision to join us after that college interview, when you were torn between this fast-paced job and the offer from a government company."

His words were a sharp reminder of the choices she had made before, of how far she had come since that first day. It was also a reminder of the respect she had for him. Navneet wasn't just a manager to her; he had been a mentor, someone whose advice she valued more than she let on. And now, hearing him lay out these options, she couldn't help but feel the weight of his belief in her.

Still, she remained quiet, her mind working overtime to process it all. What was she supposed to say to him? What could she say? She had no words in that moment, no response that would do justice to the internal storm she was fighting.

Navneet, seemingly aware of her silence, finished, "Speak to Saranya. Take your time. I think you'll make the right choice, just like the time you chose to join us." He paused, offering her a steady handshake, his gaze calm but intense. "Block out 9 a.m. on my calendar tomorrow, and let's discuss this together with Saranya."

The words hung in the air like a weight, and she nodded, acknowledging his request. "I will," she said, her voice steady despite the conflict swirling inside. She was torn, but she would give it one more thought, one more moment of clarity.

Navneet gave her a brief, understanding smile before stepping into the elevator. The doors slid shut behind him, and Magh stood there for a moment longer, her heart heavy. She finally turned toward the powder room, but the decision was still hanging over her, uncertain and looming.

She walked back from the powder room, fidgeting through her hair, lost in a chain of thoughts. She settled into her desk and resumed scrolling her emails. There was an unread email, popping up as "Exit formalities", received from her HR. The moment of truth was getting closer.

Just as Magh began sifting through the documents on her screen, a burst of laughter echoed across the floor. The chatter grew louder, light and familiar, pulling her attention away. She stood up, curious, and spotted Saranya walking in - back from her onsite project.

Saranya's hoodie read "Cape Town – where adventure awaits", but it was her radiant smile that said it all. She looked energized, fulfilled, glowing with the kind of joy that only comes from doing work that feels alive. Magh felt a sudden ache - a quiet ache of nostalgia and longing.

She remembered the day the Cape Town project was announced. The excitement among her peers, the anticipation, the hope. And then, the quiet disappointment when her name wasn't on the list. Others had gone. Others had lived the experience she had only imagined.

Saranya caught her eye and smiled warmly, gesturing that she'd come over in a few minutes. Magh nodded, returning the smile, and slowly sank back into her chair.

As she continued to go through the exit documents, she felt a quick pat on her back. It was Saranya. She invited her to go for a walk with her. Magh quickly locked her screen, gave her a side hug and started following her towards the elevator.

For the next couple of minutes in the lift, Saranya mentioned to her the different experiences of bungee jumping, road trips, living & working with different nationalities, how that exposure made her last 6 months unforgettable. They walked towards their usual Chai shop within office premises;

Saranya greeted the hawker as a long-remembered friend. He quickly recalled her and made two special ginger masala chai for them. They grabbed the cups and walked towards the park next to the shop.

As they walked side by side, Saranya nudged her playfully. "Dude, congrats on the new job," she said with a smile. "But hey… can I be honest for a second?"

Magh nodded, curious.

"When Navneet and I interviewed you back then, we had a vision," Saranya continued. "We weren't just hiring fresh grads - we were building a team, a team that would grow together, become the backbone of this place. You were always one of the strongest."

Magh looked down, unsure how to respond.

"I get it," Saranya said, taking a sip of her chai. "PKC's offering more money. That's tempting. But are you sure that's all you want? I mean… it's not exactly a fast-paced role, right? It might slow you down just when your career's picking up speed."

Magh stayed quiet, listening.

"You've got so much energy, so many ideas," Saranya added. "Why use this time to slow down? Why not build something bigger - something that's yours?"

She paused, letting the words settle.

"Look, I know the home loan's weighing on you. I really do. But what about your travel goals? Remember how excited you were about on-site opportunities? The second phase of the Cape Town project needs someone like you. I just got back, and honestly? It was amazing. I saved a ton with the per diem, got to explore, and still kept up with the work. It wasn't easy, but it was worth it."

Magh looked at her, a flicker of longing in her eyes.

"At this age," Saranya said gently, "you'll always have options. But staying, building something over time - it has its own kind of reward. I'm hitting eight years here soon. You've seen my journey. It's not perfect, but it's mine."

She smiled, warm and knowing. "Just… think about it, okay?"

Magh nodded slowly, her voice thoughtful. "I hear you. Not just you - Navneet, Taran… even more than what my dad says sometimes. I honestly don't know what the new job will bring. The onsite opportunity excites me; it really does. And I know myself - I don't want to settle into a quiet desk job. I want to build, explore, push boundaries."

She paused, her brows furrowing.

"But what if things shift in the next phase? You know how consulting works - projects change, priorities shift. What if I don't get the onsite role after all? I'll lose from both ends, won't I?"

Saranya gave a reassuring smile. "I get it. And I hear your worry. But I'm sure you'll be on that flight with us. I can even get a confirmation from the client if that helps. Let's talk to Navneet together. But only if you're truly sure - then you decide whether to take your resignation back."

The words hung in the air, heavy with possibility.

They both sipped their chai, letting the silence settle between them. No more words were exchanged as they walked back to the workspace. In the lift, the quiet felt louder than before - filled with thoughts neither of them dared to speak just yet.

As they stepped out of the lift, Saranya exclaimed, "Whatever your decision will be, choose your heart; your mind will always say run for money in the short term. Think wisely.

See you tomorrow at 9 a.m. in Navneet's cabin. I will send the meeting invitation to block his time. Sleep well and I am sure tomorrow morning's sun will give you your answer"

Magh smiled and said, "Hopefully, thanks for the chat, Saranya. Take care and see you tomorrow".

Magh walked back to her desk, her mind a whirlwind of thoughts. She took a long sip of water, trying to clear her head, before gathering her things and packing up for the day. It wasn't exactly the end of office hours, but today was different. She needed space. Time to herself. A chance to sit with her thoughts and figure out her next move.

Family. Passion. Money.

The three pillars of her life that had become tangled in her mind. She called for a cab and as it drove her home, she stared out the window, lost in thought. Navneet, Taran, Saranya, and even her dad - everyone had shared their advice, but it only made her more uncertain. The ride felt longer than it should have.

After dinner, she stepped outside with her father, Ashwani. He was a man of few words, but the wisdom in his silence was louder than anything. A middle-class man who had fought through years of hardship to provide for his family. He had seen the worst of times - when his business had crumbled, leaving him with nothing but bills and the weight of responsibility. Yet, he had always found a way. He had always kept his family afloat.

As they walked together, Magh finally broke the silence. "Dad, I'm torn. I have this opportunity for a new job. The pay's great, but my heart... I don't know if it's in it. But then again, there's this other path, one that excites me - working with the current team that I know and taking the on-site project, doing something I'm passionate about. I'm so confused."

Ashwani stopped, looking at her with the kind of understanding only a parent could have. He put his hand on her shoulder, guiding her to slow down. "Magh," he said softly, "you're asking the right questions. But remember, this is your life. You're the one who has to live with these choices. Don't let anyone else's opinions weigh you down. We've been through the toughest times, and we're still here, together. That's all that matters."

He paused, letting the words settle. "Running after money... That's a short-term fix. If you're not happy with what you're doing, the money won't mean anything. People will tell you to take the safe route. Others will say to follow your passion. But the truth is, you have to be selfish sometimes. Do what feels right for you. Because when you're at peace with your choice, you'll make everyone around you happier."

Magh felt the weight lift from her shoulders as he spoke. She looked up at him, her heart full. "I don't know what I'd do without you, Dad. You've always been my guiding force. I needed this talk more than I realized."

Ashwani smiled, his eyes twinkling with quiet pride. "Tomorrow morning, when you wake up, don't overthink it. Just focus on the first thought that comes to your mind. That'll be your answer."

Magh hugged him tightly, the weight of her uncertainty finally starting to feel lighter. "Thanks, Dad. I'm going to sleep on it tonight. I know I'll wake up with clarity."

They walked back from the colony park just outside their apartment, the cool night air surrounding them. After closing the main gate behind them, they each quietly made their way to their rooms, exchanging a simple "goodnight" as Magh noticed her mom already fast asleep.

Magh crawled into her bed, but tonight felt different. She usually preferred the darkness of her room, but tonight, she left her bedside lamp on, the soft glow of the light a subtle comfort. As she curled up beneath the blanket, her mind still raced. The usual silence of the night seemed louder, her thoughts chasing each other in circles, but her eyes slowly fluttered shut.

The next morning, her alarm buzzed at 7 a.m., jarring her from a restless sleep. She reached over and turned it off - no snooze button today. Lying still, her eyes closed, she took a few deep breaths, trying to find the clarity she had been searching for. The first thought of the day was supposed to be her answer, but as the seconds passed, she couldn't grasp it. Confused, she opened her eyes and slowly stood up. She needed to clear her head.

She walked toward the balcony, the warmth of the morning sun already beginning to filter through the curtains. As she stepped outside, the sunlight hit her face, its brightness almost startling. She blinked a few times, then, almost instinctively, glanced around. It was then that she noticed something she had seen a thousand times before but never truly looked at - the photo frame on her bedside table.

It had been there since the day her sister had gifted it to her, after her first job offer. The words "Conquer the world," printed in bold, cheerful letters, caught her eye. It was a reminder of her first steps into adulthood, into independence, but today, those words hit her differently. Something about the simplicity of those three words felt profound now. The frame had sat there for three years, but today, it seemed to pulse with a new kind of meaning.

A smile tugged at the corners of her lips, as if she was seeing those words - and herself - in a new light.

After a quick shower, she joined her dad at the breakfast table, with her favorite cucumber cheese sandwiches and freshly squeezed orange juice waiting for her. Without missing a beat, she looked up at her father and said, "Dad, I've got my answer."

Her dad smiled, pride gleaming in his eyes. "You got this, as always," he said, nodding in quiet approval.

Magh grabbed her laptop bag, stood up, and walked into the kitchen, where she hugged her mom, Reena, still basking in the warmth of the morning. She grabbed the car keys, gave a final wave to her family, and headed out the door. The decision was made.

Today would be the start of something new.

Magh had wrestled with the chaos of the Delhi-Gurgaon traffic and the thick veil of smog clinging to her rearview mirror to arrive at the office precisely at 8:55 a.m. She parked herself outside Navneet's cabin, dropping her laptop bag onto the nearest hot desk. Her fingers flicked her phone to silent as she exhaled deeply, steadying her breath.

Inside, Navneet was already mid-meeting, framed by the glass partition. His presence was as composed as ever, back straight, voice firm, likely handling a client call with the same quiet authority he was known for.

At 8:59, she spotted Saranya walking towards her, a black notebook tucked under one arm.

"Morning," Saranya greeted her with a soft smile.

"Morning," Magh replied.

At 9:01, Navneet glanced up, caught their eyes, and gave a small nod. It was time.

The two entered and took their seats opposite him.

"So," Navneet said, a mischievous glint in his eyes, "shall we talk about the on-site project while you take back your resignation?"

He chuckled lightly, but the room held a quiet tension.

Magh took a moment, collecting her thoughts. Then, calmly, she spoke.

"I've thought this through, Navneet. I've spoken to a lot of people... even my dad. I know not everyone gets this kind of opportunity, and I truly value what's on the table. But I also realized something important - whatever decision I make, it has to be for me."

She paused, her voice steady.

"Right now, I may not have complete clarity about the future, but I do know this: I want to work with leaders like you. I want to grow. And I want to explore the world too - travel has always been a dream, and no amount of money would change the fact that my mind is constantly juggling EMIs and responsibilities. In the end, I would always prioritize saving first and push my travel plans"

Navneet listened, his expression unreadable but open.

"I've decided to take the on-site opportunity," Magh continued. "I want to explore, to learn, to grow both personally and professionally. But before I withdraw my resignation, I'll need written confirmation from the client. You know how dynamic the consulting world is - I just need that assurance."

Navneet leaned back, a smile playing on his lips.

"I like how you thought about this, Magh. You're right - there's no absolute right or wrong until you live through a decision. We want our campus hires to grow with us, stay longer, and find their footing here. I spent twelve years at my first firm... and nothing after that quite matched the depth of learning I gained there."

He turned to Saranya. "Please loop in the client and CC Magh. Let's get that confirmation in writing."

"Right away, Navneet," Saranya replied, already pulling up her laptop. "We're building a stronger team."

Magh stood, offering her hand to Navneet. "Some may say I made the wrong call. Others might agree. But for the first time, I listened to myself. And I'll make sure I never regret it."

He shook her hand firmly. "Regret is always subjective, Magh. But choosing your own path and having the courage to walk it - that's what will make you stand out from the crowd."

They exchanged a smile.

Outside the cabin, Magh hugged Saranya. "Thanks for everything," she whispered.

Back at her desk, within half an hour, an email from the client landed in her inbox confirming her onboarding.

Saranya swung by, a grin on her face. "It's official. Welcome back, Magh. Go ahead and email HR about retracting your resignation."

Magh nodded, heart thumping gently. Her fingers hovered over the keyboard for a second before she began typing an email she never imagined writing three months ago. Her hands trembled slightly - but her heart didn't. For once, it felt right. Maybe not to others, but for her, it was enough.

Three weeks later, what was supposed to be a farewell party turned into a retention celebration. Magh danced under the dim lights, casting off her doubts, eyes gleaming with a quiet promise - to live a work life designed on her own terms.

P.S. Some may question Magh's choice. Others might see its wisdom. That's fair - no two paths are the same. Whether she should have taken the PKC job or not is up for debate. But in that moment, Magh did something rare - she chose herself. Her decision may not have been entirely calculated, but it was hers. And with it came peace, ownership, and the motivation to begin again.

What happens next? Well... Magh's story is just getting interesting.

CHAPTER 5

WHEN PLANS MEET REALITY

7:01 AM

Magh's alarm had barely buzzed when her phone lit up with a notification that made her sit upright.

"Resource Onboarding: MAB Bank – Mumbai."

Her heart sank. Two weeks into her new stint at ARC, this wasn't the message she'd been waiting for. No Cape Town. No passport stamps. Just a local assignment.

Still half-asleep, she grabbed her phone and dialed Saranya - no brushing, no coffee, just urgency.

"Am I going to Mumbai or Cape Town?" she asked, voice trembling.

Saranya sighed on the other end. "Good morning, Magh. There's been a delay. The Cape Town client's going through a sudden restructuring. Navneet's moved you to Mumbai with Taran - for now."

Magh froze. The dream she'd fought for, the one she'd chosen over a safer job, had just slipped through her fingers. "This isn't fair," she whispered. "I didn't take my resignation back for a local trip. People will laugh at me."

"I get it," Saranya said gently. "But this is temporary. There's a Vietnam project coming up too. We'll make sure you're considered."

Her voice carried quiet disappointment, tinged with regret. "This isn't how I imagined things would unfold," she said softly. "But I get it - this isn't in your hands."

She paused, gathering herself. "I'll speak to Navneet. I'll fight for what we agreed on. But until then, I'll do what's right. I'll go to Mumbai and see this project through."

She let out a sigh, not of defeat, but of resolve.

For two days straight, Magh spiraled. The weekend blurred into a loop of regret and frustration. She cursed her decision, vented to close friends, replayed every moment that led her to take her resignation back. The more she talked, the heavier it felt - like she'd traded her dream for a detour she never asked for.

By Sunday night, the sadness lingered like a fog. Her mom had made her favorite - Rajma rice - but Magh barely touched it. She sat at the table, spoon in hand, staring at the plate as if it held answers. It didn't.

She chewed slowly, not tasting a thing. The grief wasn't loud anymore - it was quiet, settled deep in her chest. And even though she was surrounded by comfort, she couldn't shake the feeling that she'd let herself down.

She almost broke into tears when her dad sat beside her and spoke gently.

"This is life, Magh. Don't overthink your decision. Maybe today it didn't work out the way you hoped - but who knows what's waiting down the road? Honestly, I've never been a fan of that 'everything happens for a reason' line either," he said with a wry smile. "But there's one thing I do believe in: standing by your choices. Even when they don't go as planned."

He placed a hand on her shoulder.

"Now look ahead. This Mumbai project - it's your first trip outside Delhi, managing everything on your own. That's something. Learn how to iron your clothes," he chuckled, trying to lighten the mood.

Magh didn't say much. But something softened inside her.

Two days later, a quiet smile curled on her lips. She walked back to her room, slipped under the covers, and began scrolling through her Instagram feed. The usual blur of reels and stories passed by - until one caught her eye.

Top 3 adventures to do in Cape Town.

She paused. She watched it once, then again. Her breath hitched, but she didn't cry.

Instead, she took a deep breath, unfollowed the account, and kept scrolling. The reel faded into the feed. And slowly, so did the ache.

That night, she slept - not with resolution, but with a little more peace.

Three days later, it was time. It was her time to explore a new world, maybe not how she had imagined, but it was. At 8:10 AM, she landed on her Vistara flight at the Chhatrapati Shivaji Maharaj International Airport. The word "International" was like reopening a wound she thought had healed; her heart recoiled, pierced to its core.

She looked down, switched on her phone, and started searching for an Uber.

Eight minutes later, the Uber pulled up. The driver, a man in his forties with kind cyes and a neatly pressed shirt, stepped out, hoisted her suitcase into the boot, and gave her a quick nod.

"Namaste, madam. Welcome to Mumbai," he said with a practiced smile as he slid into the driver's seat and started the engine.

Her phone buzzed. It was her mom. She answered instantly.

"Hi Mom, I've landed safely. I'll message you once I reach the hotel."

She hung up, placing the phone in her lap.

The driver glanced at her in the rearview mirror, waiting politely for the call to end.

"First time in Mumbai, madam?" he asked in a warm, curious tone.

She kept her gaze out the window, the city already beginning to blur past.

"No," she said absentmindedly - then caught herself. Her eyes focused.

"I mean… not the first time in the city. But yes, it's my first time here for work."

"Work, haan... many people come to Mumbai for that. It's the city of dreams, madam. I pray to God, may all your dreams come true here.", he replied.

The word *dreams* struck her.

For weeks, her heart had been set on Cape Town - an international project she had worked tirelessly for and imagined herself thriving in. She could almost feel the mountain breeze, the excitement of stepping into another continent, another version of herself.

Instead, here she was - living her reality in Mumbai: a two-hour flight from Delhi, monsoon humidity, and a city that moved too fast. The contrast stung. She didn't bother searching for the bigger picture. Not today. Not when the future loomed like a question she wasn't ready to ask.

She offered a faint smile, murmured a soft "Thank you" - the kind people say more out of habit than joy - and leaned back. No spark in her eyes, just a quiet surrender to the city's chaos. Closing her eyes, she braced herself for the long haul ahead. Mumbai traffic didn't move - it crawled, sighed, and sometimes, simply stood still.

An hour and a half later, the car finally pulled up outside Amara Hotel in Chembur. The sky had shifted from grey to gold, typical of Mumbai's unpredictable moods.

Her phone buzzed. A message from Taran.

"Welcome to MAB Project Magh. Settle in, have lunch, and head to the MAB Bank office. I'll loop you in once you're there."

She nodded to herself and stepped out. The Amara Hotel stood modestly tall, nestled close to the bank's head office - practical, businesslike. Just like everything about this trip. There she was on a new journey - on schedule, on assignment, and already half a world away from what she'd hoped for.

She checked into the hotel swiftly, barely exchanging pleasantries at the front desk. The room key rested in her hand; her suitcase thudded softly against the door as she entered. She unzipped it only halfway - just enough to pull out the essentials. There wasn't time or energy for more.

A quick shower washed off the fatigue of travel but not the weight she carried inside. She stepped into her business formals - the same charcoal grey suit she'd worn three years ago on her first day at work. It still fits perfectly. The smile she'd worn back then? That didn't come as easily.

Her expression in the mirror was part tired, part determined, part... grumpy. But she had no time for sentiment. She grabbed her laptop bag, phone, and slipped the room key neatly behind her phone cover - learning, slowly, how to be responsible in a way. This was her first time living away from family. Small things mattered now - like not forgetting keys or making sure her charger was packed.

She took the elevator down, her black stilettos clicking faintly against the polished floor. At the dining hall, she placed a quick order - pav bhaji. Somehow, it felt both ironic and fitting. Classic Mumbai comfort food for a day that didn't feel comforting at all.

She finished her meal quickly, not out of hunger but necessity. There was no time to savor anything today - not food, not feelings.

Stepping out of the hotel lobby, the warm afternoon air wrapped around her like a slow-burning blanket. The streets buzzed with life - vendors calling out, scooters weaving through traffic, and that unmistakable hum of Mumbai always on the move.

It was just a five-minute walk to the client's office - and two bars along the way: strategic and efficient, very Taran.

He'd planned everything down to the last detail: hotel bookings, daily schedules, even the walking route. "If you ever feel lost," he'd joked, "just follow the scent of overpriced cocktails. That's where the client's office is."

Team Delhi was lean - just the two of them: Taran and Magh, sent to kick off a high-stakes project with their Mumbai counterparts.

Taran was a curious mix: sarcastic enough to break the ice in tense meetings, yet sharp enough to slice through ambiguity like a spreadsheet ninja. He'd once told Magh, "Deadlines are like exes - ignore them and they come back nastier." But when it came to execution, he didn't miss a beat.

Magh admired that. He made work feel like a challenge, not a chore. And even though her heart still ached for Cape Town, she knew this project - with Taran - wasn't going to be dull.

Her heels clicked steadily on the pavement as she walked, the city rising around her in steel, glass, and relentless ambition. This was it - the beginning of something new. Even if her heart wasn't entirely in it yet, her feet were already moving forward.

And then, she arrived at the gate.

In bold, metallic letters, the signage read: "MAB Bank, Mumbai Branch, Chembur."

She paused for a second, almost instinctively, then walked through the glass doors.

At the reception, she followed Taran's instructions to the letter.

Visitor card - collected.

Security check - done.

Directions to the allocated workspace for Team ARC - clear in her mind.

She moved with quiet focus, making her way through the corridors, past glass-walled meeting rooms and clusters of busy employees. The city outside buzzed with chaos, but inside, everything seemed composed and controlled.

She reached the team area, spotting Taran mid-call, pacing slightly by his desk. She waited behind him, hands clasped in front, patient but alert.

He turned around, finishing the call with a curt nod, then offered a warm smile.

"Magh, welcome to Mumbai."

His tone was professional, but not cold.

He gestured to the desk behind him.

"That one's yours. Go ahead and set up. I have another meeting now, but I'll brief you right after."

As Magh placed her bag down and powered on her laptop, Taran glanced over from his screen.

"Just sent you the kick-off deck," he said casually. "Skim through it, get a feel for the flow. Oh - and try the pantry coffee. It's surprisingly drinkable... if you lower your expectations."

He smirked, then added, "We'll grab a real drink later. You've earned it just by surviving the onboarding email."

With a quick nod, he stood up. "See you in thirty."

And he left.

Exactly thirty minutes later, Taran returned - this time with another man in tow. He was short, wheatish, probably in his late forties, with a calm, experienced demeanor.

Taran gestured toward the man standing beside him. "Magh, this is Mr. Rao - the project manager from the MAB side," he said, his tone crisp but friendly.

Mr. Rao stepped forward, extending his hand with a polite smile. "Welcome to the project," he said warmly. "Looking forward to working with you."

Magh shook his hand, offering a professional nod. "Likewise, Mr. Rao. Excited to get started."

Taran chimed in with a smirk, "And don't worry, she's already survived my onboarding. She's more than ready."

They all chuckled lightly, the tension easing just enough to mark the beginning of something new.

His phone buzzed just then. He checked the screen, excused himself with a nod, and made his way back to his workspace.

The next hour was all Taran. He walked her through the scope of the project: timelines, stakeholders, expected outcomes, and of course, her role.

She listened closely, notebook open, nodding at key points. But deep inside, a quiet weight settled.

The details were clear: this wasn't a short-term fix. Despite Saranya's earlier reassurance about this being a temporary arrangement, the depth and scale of her responsibilities told a different story.

It was a long-term commitment. And she knew it.

Still, she didn't flinch. Being a professional meant showing up - mentally, emotionally, and with purpose. She promised herself to give the project her best, no matter where her dreams currently stood.

Later that evening, she walked back to the hotel with Taran. The streets of Chembur were dimly lit, the buzz of the city slowing as the day wound down.

At the hotel lobby, Taran turned to her.

"Dinner?"

She agreed with a simple nod.

They took a corner table in the dining hall and ordered two thalis - comfort food after a loaded day. Taran, ever mindful, steered clear of work talk, and she, equally careful, avoided mentioning anything about Cape Town, or the sudden shift in her plans.

But as she finished the last bite of her meal, he looked up and spoke - calmly, but with meaning.

"I'm proud of how you're handling this, Magh, really. I know this wasn't the plan. But sometimes, there's no personal choice when it comes to clients. That said..." he paused for a beat. "If any international opportunity opens up - even mid-way - I'll try to make sure you get it. But until then, I need this project to be stable. I'll look for a good replacement when the time comes."

She looked at him, caught somewhere between gratitude and quiet resignation.

She smiled - a soft, appreciative one - and nodded.

"Thanks, Taran. I will definitely make sure this project is a success."

They wrapped up dinner and walked back to their rooms, agreeing to meet at 9 a.m. sharp in the lobby.

She entered her room, her body aching from the day. Kicking off her stilettos, she pulled on her soft blue pajamas and sank into the bed.

Within seconds, sleep claimed her - proof of just how tired she was, not just physically, but in every possible way.

Eight hours later, the alarm buzzed, shrill and stubborn. She slapped the snooze button without even opening her eyes. But this time, something was different. Within seconds, her body jolted upright, heart racing.

The silence was too loud.

She looked around the unfamiliar walls of her hotel room. The light filtering through the curtain edges was cold and pale. She was alone.

Back home, Mom would've come in by now - a soft knock, a cheerful "Rise and shine," maybe even a cup of chai balanced unsteadily in one hand. But now, Mom was a few hundred kilometers away. The weight of being on her own pressed down on her chest, heavier than the duvet pooling at her waist.

She got out of bed quickly and walked to the window. Sunlight peeked through the curtains, lighting up the room. She looked outside and smiled.

A new girl in the city of dreams - ready again to make her own.

She got ready in just a few minutes and reached the lobby by 8:50 a.m. With ten minutes left before her meeting with Taran, she made a quick stop at the breakfast counter. A hot cup of chai and a sandwich in hand, she turned back toward the lobby.

There he was - waiting near the elevator, just like he said he would be.

As she walked up, she smiled and greeted him, "Good morning."

He nodded, a small smile on his face. Without saying much, they started walking together toward work.

A new journey had begun - new projects, new deadlines, new responsibilities. And somewhere deep inside, her dreams quietly shifted and grew, ready to match the rhythm of this fresh start.

Over the next two months, she threw herself into learning and soaking in new experiences. She was slowly understanding what it meant to be in Mumbai - not just the fast pace, but how to talk to Mumbaikars, whether they were clients, vendors, or even local hawkers.

She was picking up a new language - not of words, but of the working world. As a consultant, she was learning how to navigate different mindsets, very different from what she knew back in Delhi.

The project was turning out to be more than she ever expected. Taran trusted her enough to handle meetings on her own - something she'd never done before. Back in her old role, she was used to being in the background, protected under layers of management and limited responsibility.

Here, things were different. She was finally seeing what it took to handle tough clients, face their sharp questions, and still deliver under pressure. It wasn't easy. But every day, she was growing.

And then came the third month of the project. That's when she chose discomfort - stepping into the unfamiliar, doing what she had never imagined herself capable of. The previous two months had become a quiet transformation. She had started learning how to truly be with herself. She ate her meals alone without feeling awkward, managed all her expenses independently, took long walks without company, and even traveled solo within the city. Slowly, she began to find comfort in her own presence.

Then, with a mix of fear and courage, she booked her first solo trip. Even after confirming it, she found herself questioning the decision again and again - wondering if she could really go through with it. After all, she had always been a people person, surrounded by friends, family, and constant conversation. But now, something was shifting. She was learning to enjoy her own company, something she hadn't known she needed.

It's strange how we often overlook the importance of solitude when we're surrounded by the safety of our comfort zones.

But her two-month-long, unplanned crash course in self-reliance was beginning to yield quietly powerful results.

And so, there she was - a weekend before her birthday, right in the heart of the monsoon season, just one day before India's Independence Day. She landed in Sikkim, carrying a backpack and a heart full of nerves, but also something new: a sense of freedom she had never felt before.

Sikkim, a small yet breathtakingly beautiful state tucked into the northeastern Himalayas of India, felt like the perfect beginning. It was a place where nature whispered in the quiet, where snow-capped peaks stood in serene silence, and where Buddhist monasteries overlooked valleys veiled in mist. Prayer flags danced in the mountain wind, the air was crisp with peace, and time itself seemed to pause - as if the entire landscape was inviting her to slow down, listen, and simply be.

She booked a taxi from the quiet airport, and soon a local driver pulled up, stepping out to help with her bags. As he opened the boot and she began loading her backpack, he glanced around - once, then again - scanning the arrival lane.

"Is there anyone else joining?" he asked, with genuine curiosity in his voice.

She smiled softly. "No, it's just me."

He paused, his expression a mixture of surprise and mild confusion, but said nothing more as they began the drive. The car moved steadily through winding roads, the mountains rising on either side like watchful companions. For a while, they rode in silence, her eyes drinking in the shifting greens and grays of the monsoon-washed landscape.

Halfway to the hotel, he finally spoke again, this time more gently, almost hesitantly.

"Ma'am, if you don't mind me asking… have you had a fight with your family and come here?"

She turned to him, a little amused. "No, why do you ask?"

He glanced at her in the rearview mirror, still puzzled. "It's just… I've never seen anyone come alone to such a beautiful place."

She smiled again - wider this time, but not in defense. There was a quiet pride blooming inside her now. Because for once, she had chosen beauty just for herself. She was not doing it to escape anything. She was not doing it to prove anything. She was doing it just to be present with herself.

"No fight," she replied. "Just learning how to travel with my own company."

The driver nodded slowly, as if her words were taking root somewhere unfamiliar. And the road continued winding ahead, now a little quieter, a little more respectful.

She entered the hotel, checked in, and ordered dinner. After the long road journey from Bagdogra Airport to her hotel near Mall Road in Gangtok, she stepped out for a short walk. The night was quiet, and the unfamiliar city offered a strange comfort. Walking alone where no one knew her stirred a mix of vulnerability and a quiet strength. The echoes of a decision she had made months ago-the doubts, the regret-still lingered, but they no longer held her captive. Slowly, she was learning to live in the present, to understand that everything had unfolded for a reason, and to find peace in that understanding.

Over the next three days, she added new experiences to her personal journey of stepping beyond her comfort zone. Her first solo trip had been a bold choice; now, she was embracing the freedom of a no-itinerary adventure. She wandered aimlessly through Gangtok, letting the city's rhythm guide her. She admired the majestic mountains, hailed unplanned taxis to landmarks she noticed along the way, and captured spontaneous selfies.

In India, it's still uncommon to see a woman traveling alone to such scenic destinations. Her presence, independent and unaccompanied, drew curious glances. One moment, however, stood out vividly. A couple in her shared taxi to Gurudongmar Lake observed her-listening to her own music, taking selfies-and asked, "Are you a runaway bride?"

Puzzled, she asked, "Sorry, what?" Without hesitation, they repeated the question. The woman, in her thirties and wearing a beautiful red saree, explained, "We've seen news of Bengali brides who are forced into marriage and run away like this. So we were curious to ask."

Magh was taken aback. The breathtaking landscapes of Gangtok contrasted sharply with the harsh reality the couple described, a cultural backdrop where women sometimes felt compelled to escape oppressive situations. She returned to her music, but the conversation lingered in her mind.

As she continued her journey, she carried with her the awareness of these untold stories. Her solo travels were not just about personal discovery but also about recognizing the complexities and challenges faced by women in different walks of life.

Three days later, she landed back in Mumbai - the city of her new dreams. Only now, those dreams weren't distant hopes; she was living them.

In her suitcase, she carried more than souvenirs from Sikkim; she carried memories of a world she had explored all on her own, a place where silence echoed freedom, and the mountains taught her strength.

She had seen another side of life there, a quiet contrast to the stories of women she'd met along the way - young women caught in the tangle of tradition, bound by expectations, pressured into marriages they hadn't chosen.

And yet, here she was - a liberated woman, slowly waking up to the true essence of life. Every step she took now felt like an echo of those silent voices, the ones who had never been given the chance to dream.

because the life she was living… was the dream of so many others still waiting to find their wings.

After four months of relentless work, endless client meetings, chasing deadlines, and carrying the weight of accountability, she had nearly forgotten the place she once dreamed of waking up in. Her days blurred into one another, filled with the rhythm of the city and the static of a life driven by deliverables.

Then, on a rain-drenched Mumbai morning, her phone buzzed.

Navneet, the screen flashed.

Magh glanced at her new Xiaomi phone - the one she'd gifted herself on her birthday. It wasn't just a gadget. It was a symbol. A small, personal reward to mark a big milestone: her promotion to Senior Consultant.

She remembered the moment she got the news. Her heart had raced, not just with excitement, but with validation. After months of late nights, client calls that stretched into weekends, and moments of self-doubt, it had finally happened. She'd moved up.

It wasn't just a title change. It was proof that she belonged. That her voice mattered in rooms where decisions were made. That she could lead, not just follow.

She'd told no one about the tears she shed that night - happy ones, quiet ones. She'd stared at the ceiling, replaying every challenge she'd overcome. The imposter syndrome. The missed vacations. The times she'd questioned if she was cut out for this.

And now, here she was. A Senior Consultant. Still figuring things out, still learning - but standing taller.

The phone buzzed again.

Outside, the streets were already flooding. Water gushed down the roads like racing memories, vehicles honking in frustration, and yet the spirit of the Mumbaikars pulsed through the chaos: *keep going, don't look back.*

She picked up the call just as she was about to order her breakfast.

"Hi Navneet, Good Morning, How are you?" she said, brushing a damp curl from her forehead.

"I'm doing well," he replied, his voice warm and familiar. "How's Mumbai treating you?"

"It's going well," she answered, glancing out the rain-smeared window.

There was a pause - not long, but long enough to hold weight. Three seconds passed.

"Are you ready to travel for your dreams?" he asked, his tone shifting, holding something between opportunity and excitement.

"There's a project in Vietnam," he continued. "And I want you to join it. I've already discussed it with Taran. You can fly out in four weeks."

Then, with a chuckle that only deepened the gravity of the moment, he added, "As I was committed... a few months ago."

She was spellbound. For a moment, words failed her-not because she didn't want to say yes, but because it hadn't been her first dream.

She had imagined Cape Town-the view of Table Mountain rising against a pink and gold sky, the smell of ocean air drifting through open windows, a life painted in wide, wild strokes. But here she was, offered a view of the Saigon River in Vietnam instead.

Still, something had shifted in her during that solo trip-something deep. Sikkim had shown her that freedom wasn't always a place, but a feeling. A mindset. She had learned about women still fighting for the most basic choices in life. And here she was, blessed with options - two beautiful journeys laid at her feet. The luxury of choice, a dream in itself.

She took a breath and responded, her voice steady.

"Sure, Navneet. I'm ready for it. I'll make sure there's a smooth transition and I'll travel to Vietnam."

The next four weeks passed in a blur, lived as if tomorrow might never come. She threw herself into her work with relentless energy, ticking off deliverables with precision. Evenings were for farewell parties and laughter with friends, for dancing in dimly lit bars and quiet walks through familiar lanes of Mumbai, soaking in the city one last time.

Then she returned to Delhi.

Her family awaited her with open arms and bursting hearts. Her mother, glowing with both pride and quiet worry, had packed everything - Magh's favorite spices, packets of Maggi, homemade snacks wrapped with care, and quick survival recipes scribbled in a small notebook.

But beneath the warmth and welcome, there was something else. A silent hope.

Her sister Ichha had mentioned it once, casually over tea: "With this onsite opportunity, maybe we can close the home loan sooner."

It wasn't pressure. It was a belief. They saw her promotion not just as a personal win, but as a turning point for the family. A chance to breathe easier. To lighten the load.

Magh felt it in the way her mom folded her clothes with extra care, in the way her dad checked the crime rate in Vietnam late at night, and in the way Ichha asked if she'd be earning in dollars now.

She carried their dreams in her suitcase - unspoken, but heavy. And as she unpacked her bags that evening, she promised herself: I'll make this count. For me. For them.

And then came September. The day of Janmashtami, 2018. A new beginning, wrapped in tradition.

She landed in Ho Chi Minh City, Vietnam.

The air was thick, unfamiliar. Streets buzzed in a language she didn't understand. There were too many expectations swirling inside her - and just as many questions.

Will I survive here? Can I truly manage it all on my own?

But beneath the anxiety, something stronger stirred - an echo of that quiet mountain voice, from a time not long ago.

P.S. You've already begun. Just keep going.

CHAPTER 6

TIME, PRESSURE, REPEAT

"There's no blue river in the city?" Magh said, her voice quiet but tinged with disappointment, as she slid into the back seat of the cab. Her colleague had come to pick her up from the airport, cheerful and ready, but she was still adjusting to the change in air, in light, in pace.

Harit smirked from the front seat without turning around. "This isn't Cape Town, Magh," he teased. "Did you even Google this place before landing?" He chuckled, then added, "It's an international project, sure, but doesn't quite feel like living abroad, does it?"

Magh didn't answer right away. Her gaze wandered to the windows, watching Ho Chi Minh City blur past - scooters weaving like thread through traffic, street vendors fanning the smoke from skewers, flashes of neon and tangled wires stretching across the skyline.

Harit kept talking, his voice relaxed, as he pointed out landmarks along the way. He was broad-chested, fair-skinned, and dressed head-to-toe in a black Adidas tracksuit - someone who looked like he belonged in any city, anywhere.

"I didn't really research," Magh finally replied, her tone thoughtful. "I'm just... going with the flow, seeing where life takes me, and learning, slowly, to acknowledge the freedom of choices, the kind some only dare to dream of."

Harit gave a knowing smile. "Vietnam might not be the dream you had in mind, but you'll see - it has its charm. We've built a great team here. Feels more like a family now. And there are some beautiful places nearby we all explore when we can. You're part of that now."

Forty minutes later, as the sky dipped into evening hues, the cab pulled up in front of their accommodation. A gust of hot, dense air greeted her as she stepped out. Before her stood Skyon Apartments - a modern condominium rising tall amidst the bustle. A familiar 7-Eleven sat just across the entrance, flanked by tiny shops and the buzz of life.

Harit helped her unload her suitcases and led her to her assigned unit. Each team member had been given a studio, compact yet self-contained. When she opened the door, Magh paused. A soft smile crept across her face.

The studio wasn't luxurious, but it had soul. An island kitchen stood at the center, clean white walls bathed in warm evening light. An antique dining table sat in the corner, and a white IKEA bed awaited her like a quiet invitation. It didn't feel like home, nor quite like a hotel. But it was hers - and that was enough. It felt freeing.

Harit gave her a quick rundown of the basics: the WiFi password, the laundry schedule, how to sort the garbage. Then, he pointed toward the covered dish on the counter. "The team cooked dinner and saved some for you. We placed it earlier in your apartment."

Magh blinked, touched. The warmth of that small gesture settled into her chest.

"Thank you," she said, sincerely. "Really."

Harit nodded and made his way to the door. "Meet me in the lobby tomorrow at 8:50. The client's office is just a ten-minute walk."

"Got it," she said, and closed the door behind him.

She unpacked only what she needed, called her family to let them know she'd arrived safely, and ate dinner slowly, savoring the quiet. After a quick shower, she slipped under the covers of her king-size bed, curled up tight, and closed her eyes.

Her first night in a new country. Unknown streets. Familiar faces. And for the first time in a long while, Magh felt a little less lost.

At 8:00 am, the shrill buzz of her alarm sliced through the morning stillness. She sprang from bed, her feet brushing the cool floor as she approached the window. Beyond the glass, Saigon unfurled - a mosaic of glass towers and the winding Saigon River, bathed in the soft glow of dawn. It was the moment she'd longed for: waking up in a new city, adding another flag to her travel diary, and calculating her per diem with meticulous care. Each cent saved was a step closer to balancing family obligations with her dream of exploring the world.

She inhaled deeply, savoring the rising sun's warmth on her skin. Dressed in a tailored ocean-blue suit, she felt the weight of her aspirations settle comfortably on her shoulders. As she stepped out, the city greeted her with its unique rhythm.

In the lobby, Harit was waiting, his presence a reassuring constant. He led her to BWC bank's towering headquarters, its sleek façade gleaming just around the corner from her apartment. Registration was swift; the vendor pass would come later, but today, she was a visitor, an observer.

They strolled down the hallway, passing a modest Vietnamese shop. The air was thick with the aroma of sizzling pho and freshly baked bánh mì. Harit smiled, pointing to a chilled coconut water. "Best in the team," he said. She followed his lead, adding a sandwich to her order.

With each bite and sip, she felt more connected to this vibrant culture, more attuned to its pulse. They entered the elevator together, ascending to the eighth floor, where her new journey awaited.

Magh stepped into the team's bay, greeted by a chorus of smiles and nods. Some colleagues glanced up, offering a quick "Hi," before returning to their screens. Others, more curious, asked, "What made you join this project?" "If you're a workaholic, this place is heaven," one chuckled, half in jest.

While the banter was light, Magh sensed an undercurrent of tension among the junior team members. Perhaps it was too early to judge, but she couldn't shake the feeling that all was not as it seemed.

The atmosphere shifted abruptly as Kapil, the new senior manager, entered. Dressed in a sharp black suit, he was a recent hire on the team. Short in stature, fair-skinned, and seemingly in his mid-forties, he made no attempt to greet the team. Without a word, he walked straight to his cabin.

An invisible wall seemed to descend over the bay. The energy drained from the room as everyone became engrossed in their work, faces set in concentration. It was as if they were all following an unspoken directive to work silently and efficiently.

She found her desk, marked with a sticky note bearing her name. She unpacked her laptop, plugged it in, and began to settle in.

Moments later, Bhavna, her reporting manager, approached. "Welcome to the project," she said with a warm smile. "We were waiting for you to join. I hope you wrapped up things well in Mumbai. Taran mentioned he might still need some of your time, but I think you can manage."

Bhavna handed her a presentation. "This outlines the client's challenge. I want you to design a business solution. Take today to talk to the team and explore the datasets. Harit can assist you with access and any other resources you need. Don't hesitate to tap me on the shoulder if you need anything."

Magh returned the smile and offered a firm handshake. "Thanks for the warm welcome. I'll dive into this and get back to you."

As Bhavna returned to her desk, Magh opened the documents, ready to immerse herself in the task ahead.

The floor was silent - unnaturally so. It felt less like an office and more like a strict classroom, where no one dared to speak unless it was about work. Magh glanced around, trying to read the expressions and posture of her colleagues, but they were buried in their screens, mechanical in their focus. For the next hour, the only energy she could sense was tension. Her juniors sat side by side, hunched over, as if crushed beneath invisible weights-deadlines, expectations, directionless tasks. They reminded her of mechanics trying to fix a machine with no blueprint.

Client stakeholders drifted in and out, stopping by desks with clipped conversations - some voicing disappointment, others clearly disagreeing with the team's trajectory. The air felt colder after every such exchange.

Three and a half hours passed.

At precisely 12:30 pm, Magh noticed a curious sight: a large group of Vietnamese employees stood up all at once. It was so synchronized, it felt like someone had blown a whistle. They began filing out, quiet but purposeful.

"They're leaving for lunch," Harit said, catching the look of surprise on Magh's face. "Happens every day, on the dot."

Thirty minutes later, hunger nudged her. She looked around, expecting someone to suggest a break. But her team stayed glued to their screens, unmoving. No one even looked up.

Then Bhavna walked in, her presence breaking the stillness.

"Guys, go grab lunch," she said.

A few looked up, hesitating. One muttered, "I will join in a while." The rest said nothing.

Bhavna turned to Magh. "Come on, let's go."

Magh followed her and Harit to a nearby shop where they picked up vegetarian bánh mì – Bhavna's treat to welcome her. On their way back, she saw something that made her smile. A few employees from the client side were already done with lunch, curled up with plushies, their knees hugged to their chest, catching a quick nap.

Bhavna noticed her amusement. "That's the culture here. One-hour lunch breaks. Half an hour for food, half for rest. They slurp their pho, then power nap."

Magh chuckled. "Honestly, that's... refreshing. A break like that must be amazing for productivity - and mental health too. Why don't we do that?"

Harit laughed, dry and bitter. "We wish. Getting time to eat at all feels like a luxury some days."

Magh didn't press further. Her expression said enough.

Back at the office, she unwrapped her sandwich and tried to focus. But her heart wasn't in it. Like everyone else, she ate at her desk, eyes still on the screen - another cog in the machine.

As the hours slipped by, the monotony began to shift. Magh noticed some colleagues forming small groups-some sneaking in quick breaks, others shuffling off to meetings. Despite the motion, the atmosphere remained dull, as if a weight hung over them all. There was a team here, yes - but one drained of spirit.

At exactly 6:30 pm, the senior manager, Kapil, stepped out of his cabin. He approached Bhavna, speaking in low tones. Magh couldn't hear the words, but she could read the shift in Bhavna's face - the glow she carried earlier dimmed. She nodded slowly, her expression tight, and returned quietly to her desk. Kapil left soon after, briefcase in hand.

And then, as if someone had released a held breath, the energy in the room shifted.

Postures relaxed. Someone laughed - just a little at first - then a few giggles turned into full conversations. A teammate asked, "What's the plan for dinner?" Another stretched, letting out a long sigh of relief. It struck Magh how much pressure had been tethered to Kapil's presence - and to the client expectations hovering invisibly in the air. With him gone, they were suddenly human again. For the first time that day, they resembled the idea of a team she had hoped to join - talking, laughing, sharing lightness in the cracks of a heavy job.

She heard murmurs of stress: how overwhelming the pace had become, how badly some needed a drink. It was only Monday.

It was still early to judge, she reminded herself, but Magh felt she was slowly starting to understand the rhythm of the place. She was beginning to find her footing.

Some colleagues headed back to the apartment complex, while a few made impromptu plans to grab dinner and drinks near the walking street. Magh chose to follow Harit and Bhavna.

To her surprise, they landed at a cozy Indian restaurant tucked into the neighborhood. She hadn't expected it, but it turned out to be the team's favorite. Over steaming plates of food, they relaxed into an easy togetherness. Magh ordered her comfort dish - daal khichdi - and it felt like a soft landing after a long, unsure day.

As she listened, the dinner conversation drifted between light gossip and heavier concerns about timelines and workload. Magh remained quiet, taking it all in. It was only her first day - too soon to weigh in, and too early to judge the book by its cover.

They finished dinner and walked back, the warm night air brushing their faces. On the way, Harit and Bhavna pointed out a few local landmarks - the glow of Ho Chi Minh City felt distant yet welcoming.

Fifteen minutes later, they reached their condominium. At the gate, everyone bade each other goodnight. Someone called out, "Don't work tonight, get some rest," and a few nodded in agreement.

Back in her room, Magh kicked off her shoes and called the one person who'd been waiting to hear about her day - her mom. Her ever-patient listener.

She recounted everything: the quiet tension, the lunch nap culture, the dinner outing. Her words slowed, her voice softened with fatigue.

After hanging up, she set an alarm, washed her face, and crawled into bed. As she curled up beneath the blanket, the questions still lingering in her mind slowly faded into dreams.

Over the next month, the pressure only built. It wasn't a sudden storm - it came down like a slow, steady cascade. Magh found herself in daily meetings with the client, Kapil, and other project managers. The client's stakeholders were blunt, almost cold. To them, the team wasn't a group of professionals - they were vendors. They were names attached to deadlines and task lists. Empathy wasn't part of the conversation.

By mid-November, Navneet flew into Vietnam for a high-level meeting with the CEO of BWC Bank. Later that evening, he joined the team for a quick catch-up, a hallmark of his leadership style: staying connected, checking in, making people feel seen.

He greeted the room warmly and asked casually, "Is anyone getting time to work out? Is anyone using the gym at the condo?"

No one answered right away.

One colleague finally said, "There's no time."

Two others - including Magh - offered, "We try to get at least 30 minutes on the treadmill."

Navneet nodded thoughtfully, then spoke in a calm but firm tone.

"We all get 24 hours in a day," he said. "If you're telling me we can't spare even 60 minutes for ourselves, then we're clearly running this project-and this team-the wrong way. If you can't take care of yourself, your ability to contribute meaningfully to work is going to suffer too."

The room was quiet. The boardroom's glass walls reflected a team worn thin. Kapil and a few other senior managers were not in the meeting room, but their presence, and the pressure they left behind, still lingered like a shadow.

Navneet looked around. "If you can't share with me what's really going on, I can't help," he said.

Still, no one spoke.

He let the silence hang for a few moments, then gave a soft sigh and stood.

"All right," he said with a smile, trying to lift the mood. "Let's go out for drinks."

Later that evening, they arrived at a stunning Mediterranean restaurant, glowing with warm lights and live music. The venue had been pre-booked by Navneet's assistant - a thoughtful touch that hinted at the leader who still believed in people, even when they'd forgotten how to believe in themselves.

As the party got underway, Navneet scanned the room. Almost instantly, the team fragmented; leaders clustered near the buffet, the newly promoted managers claimed a corner near the bar, and the junior teammates huddled by the windows. He sighed. So much for team bonding.

Still, he gave it a try. He clinked his glass gently for attention and spoke a few words about teamwork, collaboration, and how each of them mattered. They listened politely, smiled, nodded, and then quietly returned to their own circles.

Magh, standing among the juniors, caught bits of a conversation spiraling into a familiar rant about work pressure. The kind of talk that rarely left the room but lingered in people's heads.

Meanwhile, Harit hesitated, then made up his mind. He walked over to Navneet, something clearly weighing on him.

"Hey, do you have a minute?" he asked, eyes clouded.

"Of course," Navneet said, stepping aside with him.

Harit opened up, not just about the last few weeks, but the months of feeling unheard, of carrying stress that seeped into his work. Navneet listened. Fully. No interruptions, no defensiveness, just quiet, present attention.

When the conversation ended, a faint smile flickered on Harit's face, something Magh hadn't seen in a long while.

It didn't go unnoticed. One by one, five more teammates approached Navneet, each with their own stories, frustrations, and questions. He received them all without hurry. He didn't offer instant fixes. No platitudes or sugarcoated answers. Just honest listening and a calm reassurance: "We'll work through this. But I want to understand more before we can spin this around for a better working environment."

That night, Navneet didn't solve the team's problems. But he did something just as rare - he made them feel heard. And in that, the seed of change was planted.

Later that night, as the party thinned out and the laughter softened into murmurs, Magh walked up to Navneet, who was still laughing at a joke someone had cracked.

"Hey… can I have a minute?" she asked quietly.

His smile faltered, curiosity replacing amusement. "Sure. But you just joined the team. Do you already have concerns?"

Magh shook her head. "It's not about me. It's about the team."

That made him pause. His expression shifted, less guarded now, more open. Someone new noticing something was often more telling than those who'd been around too long to see it anymore.

He nodded. "Let's step outside."

The restaurant patio was quieter, the city humming softly in the distance. He turned to her. "All right. I'm listening."

Magh took a breath, steadying her voice.

"I've come to you for solutions before for myself, Navneet. But tonight… maybe it's not for me. It's for them. The team. I've only been here a few weeks, but what I'm seeing, it's worrying me every day."

She looked at him, her eyes sincere.

"For the past two months, they've been working like machines. Staying late, eating dinner at their desks, heading home just long enough to sleep a few hours before doing it all over again. And they're not just tired-they're drained. No spark. No direction. I rarely see them smile anymore."

Navneet said nothing. He looked down, thoughtful, resting his fingers against his mouth, fidgeting, and listening harder than most would notice.

"I don't know if it's the pressure, or if the leadership's just too stretched to notice. Maybe everyone's doing their best. But… whatever it is, the junior team - they're not okay. And I'm scared this is starting to affect their health too. It will slowly impact me too."

The silence hung between them for a moment, heavy but honest.

Navneet finally exhaled. He didn't speak yet, but the shift in his posture, the quiet urgency in his eyes, said enough. He was thinking. Deeply. Not just about what to fix, but how to truly change something.

Navneet looked up slowly, his brows knit in quiet concern. "What do you think they need, Magh? You're the closest to them right now."

Magh hesitated. She hadn't expected the question. She looked away for a second, collecting her thoughts.

"I don't know what would really change things," she said softly. "But… Being heard matters. Feeling seen. Even if appraisals aren't around the corner, a few words of appreciation may help them a long way. Some kind of real motivation. Not just tasks and deadlines, but also being treated with respect."

She paused, her voice gaining weight.

"They're not asking for miracles. Just to be treated like humans. Right now, it feels like… they're being run to the ground. As if they're only worth the hours they clock in. I know there's pressure from the client. I get it. But leadership should be a shield, not another layer of the storm."

She looked back at him, her throat tightening.

"It should feel like us versus the client. Not one junior versus everyone above them."

Her voice cracked, just slightly. She didn't try to hide it, she knew sooner or later she would be in the same boat.

Navneet was quiet for a long beat, his eyes on her but his mind clearly turning over what she'd said. Then he nodded.

"Thank you for being this honest with me," he said, the gravity in his voice unmistakable. "We need to change the tone. The atmosphere. And I want to start tonight."

He stood straighter, a hint of resolve returning to his expression. "Let's organize an after-party. Not at a restaurant. At one of our apartments. No managers. No senior leads. No talk of the project. Just the team, relaxed. I want to see them outside this structure… where they can just be themselves."

Magh blinked. "But don't you have a flight tomorrow morning?"

Navneet smiled faintly, a spark of conviction in his eyes. "Yeah. I do."

He looked out at the dark sky, then back at her.

"But this is important."

Magh leaned in, her eyes lighting up with a sudden idea. "How about a poker night?"

Navneet didn't even blink. "Let's do it."

No corporate hesitation, no need to 'circle back.' Just a clear, instant yes. That was all she needed.

They stepped back into the restaurant, the music still playing low, groups still clustered in their silos. Without a word, they split - Navneet heading toward the senior leads to quietly excuse himself, and Magh making a beeline for the junior table.

She leaned over and grinned. "Guess what? Poker night. Tonight. Navneet wants in."

There was a pause. Then a few groans.

"Oh God, no," someone muttered. "We'll end up talking about project deadlines over cards."

"Yeah," another added, "the last thing we need is work stress and losing poker chips to our seniors."

Magh held up her hands, silencing them. "Guys, shhh, he's not inviting the senior leads. It's just us. Him and the team. No hierarchy. No meetings. Just poker."

The skepticism lingered for a moment, but slowly, curiosity began to replace resistance. One by one, heads nodded.

"All right," Harit said, a rare smirk tugging at his lips. "I'm in."

An hour later, the restaurant lights dimmed behind them and the laughter shifted into a new space - Harit's apartment.

Shoes came off at the door. Laptops stayed zipped. Tracksuits and pajamas replaced office formals, and the familiar scent of takeout filled the air.

They sat on the floor, circling around a makeshift table - just an old rug and a worn deck of cards in the center. Laughter returned, genuine this time, light and unguarded. And sitting there with them, cross-legged like everyone else, was Navneet. No title, no airs. Just one of them.

He didn't command the room. He didn't lead the game. He simply joined it.

In that small, unplanned moment, something shifted. The team wasn't just seen - they were equal. And for the first time in a long time, they weren't "resources" or roles on a slide deck.

They were just people. Together.

The night stretched late, but not because of the cards. The real wins came in the form of laughter - unfiltered and long overdue. The poker chips may have changed hands, but what lingered was a sense of ease none of them had felt in months.

The next morning, as the city stirred awake, Harit's phone buzzed.

It was Navneet.

"Hey, are you free to meet me at the coffee shop? Just a minute's walk from your place. I thought we could chat before I head out."

Harit rubbed his eyes, still half-asleep, and replied with a simple "Sure." A few minutes later, he stepped into the cozy corner café down the street. Navneet was already there, a half-finished cappuccino in front of him, his posture relaxed but alert.

What Harit thought would be a quick check-in turned into a thoughtful exchange. Navneet asked, listened, and noted. Not with a manager's lens - but like someone trying to piece together a bigger picture, one voice at a time.

Over the next few hours, each junior team member received a similar message. One by one, they walked to the café, had their fifteen minutes, and left with something lighter in their expression. Meanwhile, Magh's apartment became the waiting lounge - a space of anticipation and quiet reflection.

Later, the senior leads were also seen walking toward the café. The dynamic had shifted: it wasn't top-down anymore. It was person to person.

Back at Magh's, the juniors regrouped. Someone brewed tea. Another passed around leftover chips from the night before.

"So? What did you say?" Harit asked, looking around.

They shared bits and pieces - some opened up about the burnout, some spoke of team morale, others just offered their perspective. A few remained quiet, uncertain if it would lead anywhere.

"I don't think much will change," one of them shrugged. "It's the system, after all."

"Maybe," Magh said softly, "but this is the first time someone even asked."

There was a pause. Then a nod. Then another.

As Navneet packed his bags and headed to the airport, his thoughts weren't just on his flight. They were with the voices he'd heard that morning - some tired, some uncertain, but all honest.

And somewhere in that collection of stories, concerns, and small hopes, something had sparked.

Not a solution.

But a beginning.

Monday morning rolled in with its usual sluggishness, but something felt… off.

The junior team's group chat buzzed unexpectedly. A message, short and sweet, pinged just as the sun crept in through dusty window blinds:

They stared at the screen.

"Did he just say coffee for us in the other group chat? I think my stomach would die?" Harit typed in the group without the managers.

A few laughing emojis followed, the digital equivalent of rolling eyes. Nobody really believed it. Most thought it was a classic case of "buttering the goat before the slaughter."

Only Bhavna replied in the main group, her tone carefully respectful - a subtle nod to the senior manager's gesture. No one else said a word.

The office filled up slowly, as it always did. Keyboards clicked, deadlines loomed, and hustle returned to its usual madness.

Then entered Kapil.

He walked in, quieter than usual, holding a large brown bag as if it carried something sacred. He placed it in the middle of the white center table and called out, voice calm but clear:

"Coffee, team. Please help yourselves. Let's have our stand-up an hour later today. Just… enjoy your coffee first."

Silence.

Glances shot across desks. Eyes met, then darted away. Sarcastic smirks curled lips. A few thoughts danced in unison:

What happened to the boss?

Did Navneet finally give him a taste of his own medicine?

Some reached for the coffee out of habit. Others stayed glued to their screens, pounding the keys a bit harder.

Bhavna walked over, a cup in hand, and paused near the juniors. She leaned in just enough for them to hear, voice low but firm.

"Guys, if someone's trying to change… maybe let's try being supportive."

There was a moment. A beat.

A few nodded, and slowly, one by one, more hands reached for the coffee.

Maybe it wasn't just caffeine in the air. Maybe it was the start of something else.

The following weeks didn't bring a revolution, but something had shifted.

It wasn't loud or dramatic. No fireworks, no big announcements. Just… quieter meetings. Softer tones. Fewer sarcastic glances when someone from the senior team spoke.

The juniors noticed.

The communication, once sharp, mechanical, and cold, now carried a little more thought, a little more space to breathe. The constant sense of being watched, of being treated like cogs in a machine, had eased. Not vanished, but softened.

One evening, after yet another long day of pushing code and dodging deadlines, a message popped up in Navneet's inbox.

"Thanks for hearing us out. It meant more than we could say back then."

Another followed not long after.

"If all leaders could be like you… we'd be finishing projects, not just surviving them."

Navneet smiled at his screen. He didn't reply right away. He rarely did. He knew when to let words settle.

The next day, another message came in - this time from Magh, short and honest:

"The team is doing better. I just thought you should know."

Navneet responded the next day.

"Things can be better when we choose positivity. Your seniors - they're human too. They're learning. We all are."

Magh read the message twice, then once more. It wasn't just a line. It was a reminder.

P.S: Change didn't need to be loud to be real. Sometimes, it slips in quietly - through shared cups of coffee, silent realizations, and the courage to speak up, even when it feels like no one's listening.

As the days rolled by, the chaos of the initial transition began to settle. Some days felt smoother, lighter. Others still carried the weight of the past. Slowly, the team found its rhythm. Every couple of weeks, they'd gather for lunch with the senior members - small moments that hinted at connection, even if a quiet divide lingered. It wasn't always spoken, but it was there - a line drawn not on the table, but somewhere in their minds.

In the months that followed, a few team members took it upon themselves to break the routine. They planned weekend escapes to nearby gems: Da Nang, Hoi An, Hanoi. Beautiful places that whispered of freedom. Even with looming deadlines, some chose to prioritize themselves - sneaking in gym sessions, or spontaneous road trips that made Monday mornings a little more bearable.

Magh was quietly carving out her own version of a dream - not in Cape Town as she once imagined, but in this vibrant corner of Vietnam. She was learning to stand on her own, to enjoy her solitude. Morning walks through buzzing streets, sipping egg coffee alone at a quiet café - not out of loneliness, but choice. She had begun to tell her colleagues, kindly but firmly, "I need this time with myself." In those small acts, she was becoming her own person-discovering how to love herself first.

As the year drew to a close, excitement stirred quietly among the team. Conversations drifted from deadlines to destinations, and many - including Magh - began tucking away their per diem, saving up for a well-deserved New Year's escape.

Magh eventually found herself joining Harit and two of the younger teammates on a trip to Hoi An - the enchanting city of lanterns. It felt fitting, almost poetic, to end the year wrapped in color and light.

On Christmas Eve - her favorite time of year - Magh boarded a flight to Da Nang. That evening, she wandered the soft edges of the beach, letting the sound of waves wash over the noise in her head. It was a quiet celebration, but it felt right. The next morning, with a heart full of calm and a small bag packed, she caught a cab to Hoi An. The journey was simple, but the anticipation shimmered - like the lanterns waiting to be lit.

Hoi An welcomed Magh like a quiet song - gentle, old-world, and somehow familiar. The yellow-washed walls of ancient houses, draped with bougainvillea, lined narrow streets where bicycles glided past and the scent of incense mingled with fresh bread. It was a place that seemed to pause time, letting visitors breathe slower, deeper.

For the next few days, Magh wandered the city on her own terms. She slipped into quiet cafés with creaky wooden chairs and soft jazz humming in the background. Sometimes she walked around, sometimes she just watched the world pass by - locals bargaining in the market, children running barefoot, lanterns swaying lazily in the afternoon breeze. No one expected anything of her here. And for once, she didn't expect too much from herself either.

On the New Year's Eve, she walked down to the river, where the lantern stalls glowed in soft pinks, golds, and violets. She picked one - delicate, sky blue - and lit it with trembling fingers. Holding it close for a moment, she whispered, no wish aloud. There was just a silent promise to herself. Then, with a breath of release, she let it fly - watching it rise into the warm sky, joining a constellation of hopes flickering in the dark.

It wasn't just a ritual. It felt like letting go of something old, something heavy. In that moment, with her bare feet on the cool earth and a river of light above her, Magh tasted something she hadn't felt in a long time: freedom - not the kind that comes with distance from work or people, but the kind that blooms when you belong to yourself.

She would return to her life in Ho Chi Minh soon. But something had shifted. She had taken these days and made them hers - simple, imperfect, luminous.

Magh welcomed 2019 with a quiet smile and a heart full of light. From the balcony of her homestay, she gazed down at the morning bustle of the market below - the same streets that had glowed with lanterns and laughter just hours before. The city, now bathed in golden sunlight, felt like it was waking up gently, just as she was.

She took a deep breath, letting the crisp air fill her lungs, and whispered a soft prayer of gratitude for this journey, for the dreams she was living, for a moment of clarity, for a memory of freedom, and for a sense of her own becoming.

She packed her bags slowly, savoring the last few moments in the room that had become her sanctuary for the last few days. Down in the lobby, she reunited with Harit and the others. Together, they headed to the airport, the hum of reality gradually returning.

Back in Ho Chi Minh City, the rhythm picked up again. The workdays were full - sometimes frenzied, sometimes fulfilling. But something had shifted in her. The chaos didn't rattle her the same way. She had begun to see beauty in the hustle - the quick meetings, the shared laughter over lunch, the quiet pride in a task well done.

Evenings in her apartment were still. She had carved a space for herself there - a small corner by the window, her favorite mug, playlists that felt like home. Sometimes, in the silence, the ache of missing her family would rise, sharp and sudden. It pinched, yes. But it also reminded her of the love waiting oceans away. Somehow, that made her stronger.

She was still learning - about the world, about work, about herself. Magh wasn't just surviving.

She was growing.

A few days after returning from Hoi An, life had settled back into its usual pace. Morning stand-ups, project updates, coffee breaks - it all felt familiar again. But on that particular morning, as the stand-up wrapped up, Bhavna approached Magh with a strange stillness in her eyes.

"Magh, can you join me for a coffee?" she asked quietly.

They walked together to the pantry in silence, the hallway suddenly feeling longer than usual. As they reached the corner table, Bhavna finally spoke - her voice low and slightly shaken.

"Magh… we have to send you back to India in the next two weeks."

The words hung in the air, heavy and cold.

Magh stood still, the warmth from her coffee cup suddenly distant. It felt like the floor beneath her had shifted. She had always known Vietnam was temporary, but she hadn't expected the ending to arrive so suddenly, like the final scene of a movie she wasn't ready to finish.

"What happened, Bhavna?" Her voice trembled, barely holding itself together.

Bhavna sighed, choosing her words carefully. "The project will continue as planned, but the client and leadership have decided to reduce the onshore team size due to ongoing delays. They'll provide remote access from India, but..." she trailed off, the rest left unsaid.

Magh had heard whispers of this a month ago - three juniors had been sent back without much explanation. At the time, it had seemed distant, unlikely. Now, it was personal.

Her mind raced. The late-night city walks, the egg coffees, the weekend trips, the independence she had started to build - all of it flashed before her eyes like postcards from a dream that was being folded away too soon.

She nodded slowly, holding her expression still. "Okay, Bhavna. If that's the client's call... then that's how it goes." A faint smile - almost bitter - curved at her lips. "It's always the client's plan above ours, right?"

Without waiting for a response, she turned and walked back to her desk.

Two weeks later, she boarded a flight back to India. Her suitcase was heavier this time - not just with souvenirs, but with stories, scents, lessons, and quiet courage. She stared out of the window as the plane took off, the lights of Ho Chi Minh flickering below like goodbye notes.

She wasn't disappointed anymore. She was just reflective and happy that it happened. The life she had started to build here had been real. And it mattered.

As the clouds parted below her, a quiet conviction grew in her chest: This isn't the end.

P.S. She had only just begun. The dream didn't end in Vietnam. It had only changed shape.

CHAPTER 7

THINKING OUT OF THE "BOX"

The echo of dhol beats and laughter from the Lohri celebration still lingered in her mind. That weekend had been a warm escape - wrapped in bonfires, family, and old comfort. But as the New Year of 2019 began, so did the relentless rhythm of routine.

She stepped onto the metro at HUDA City Centre, the cold metallic doors closing behind her with a mechanical finality. The train hummed forward, dragging her back into the loop of city life.

Seated across from her, Adira noticed the faraway look in her friend's eyes. Adira, her closest college friend and her new travel partner to Gurgaon, had recently joined another company near her office.

"How was your work trip to Ho Chi Minh?" she asked, nudging her lightly.

Magh smiled, but it didn't reach her eyes. "Six months of walking ten minutes to work, quick weekend getaways, no two-hour-one-way commute… it felt like a dream in itself that she lived."

"You are still missing the fragrance of the famous Pho?" Adira laughed and asked, adjusting the strap of her laptop bag.

Magh let out a breath that carried more than just exhaustion. "I didn't realize how much I had until I came back. I feel privileged to get such an opportunity. There, I had time. Time to cook, to read, but at the same time I used to miss my family and friends. So, there are pros and cons of wherever you are."

They both fell silent as the metro rushed past stations, each stop a reminder of distance - not just in miles, but in lifestyle.

"Now that you're back," Adira said gently, and you've got plans. New year. Any new goals planned already?"

Magh looked out the window at the blur of buildings and thought of her notebook pages already filled with goals, to-dos, and dreams waiting for space.

"Yeah," she nodded slowly. "Similar task list, different city, yet it's my own."""

Adira nodded, offering a quiet smile as the train rocked gently beneath their feet. "You will do great, Magh, just like our college days," she said, her voice steady over the low murmur of announcements and the rhythmic clatter of the metro tracks.

Fluorescent lights flickered overhead, casting a sterile glow on the metal poles and worn plastic seats. Outside the window, the city blurred into streaks of concrete and neon, a fast-moving canvas of everyday life.

Magh leaned back against the glass, her eyes thoughtful as she traced the outline of a faded travel sticker on her backpack. "That's the souvenir from Ho Chi Minh," she said with a half-smile, "a little reminder that I'm still chasing my travel dreams - just juggling them with my corporate task list."

A vendor's call echoed from a nearby station platform as the train slowed to a stop. For a moment, the world outside seemed to hold its breath - just long enough for two friends to anchor themselves in each other's words, before the journey carried them forward again.

As the metro slid to a halt at the office station and they walked together towards the office lobby, Magh turned to Adira with a parting smile. "Bye. Have a good one," she said warmly, watching Adira walk to the tower behind her office building.

Magh entered the elevator, which chimed softly as it opened on the fifth floor. Back to basics, she thought. The familiar hum of the office greeted her, blending with the faint aroma of freshly brewed coffee and photocopier ink.

As she stepped onto the floor, her eyes instinctively landed on Navneet's cabin, the space that once held a different kind of tension. A flicker of memory-her resignation discussion from months ago-flashed across her mind like a snapshot caught in motion. She shook it off and moved swiftly to grab a hot desk at the far end of the bay, intentionally placing distance between herself and the glass-walled office.

Just as she began unpacking her things, fingers poised to switch on her laptop, a familiar voice cut through the hum of the workspace.

"Magh!"

She turned to see Saranya, her eyes wide with warmth. "How are you, dude? How were things in Vietnam?"

Magh's face lit up. The weight she hadn't realized she was carrying eased slightly at the sight of a familiar friend.

She stepped toward Saranya, her voice full of quiet pride and excitement. "It was amazing. I've come back with so many new experiences... and new dreams."

Her words spilled out with a gentle rhythm, "Over the last year, traveling between Mumbai and Vietnam, going on solo trips, working with people from different nationalities, immersing myself in new cultures-it all changed me. It's been a journey of challenges, freedom and self-discovery. It filled my bag with stories… and it has made me a new person who enjoys her own company and values the experiences she gets."

Around them, the office buzzed with the usual Monday noise, but for a moment, Magh stood rooted in something deeper: growth, gratitude, and the promise of a new beginning in familiar territory.

Saranya's face lit up with a broad smile, her eyes crinkling at the corners. She couldn't help but think back to the decision Magh had made months ago-the leap of faith, the bold move-and how right it had turned out. There was no trace of regret in her expression, only pride.

"Come on," she said, nudging Magh playfully. "Let's go grab chai. You have to share all the gossip with me. About all those adventures you had in Vietnam, on your solo trips, everything. Over chai, of course!"

Magh laughed, the tension of the morning finally beginning to melt. "Absolutely. But chai's on me today," she grinned, slinging her tote over her shoulder. "I managed to save a decent chunk from the per diems - one of the perks I was excited about. I also made a big EMI payment for my house loan recently with the savings."

They both chuckled as they walked toward the pantry, the clatter of keyboards and distant phone calls fading behind them. The scent of cardamom and office bustle mingled in the air - an ordinary setting made extraordinary by stories waiting to be told.

For the next month, Magh nestled herself into the comforting warmth of home - lazy breakfasts over weekends with her parents, late-night laughs with cousins, familiar lanes echoing with childhood memories. She was content, or at least she told herself so. But a part of her remained tethered to the world she had just stepped out of.

Every day, she'd scroll through chats from her Ho Chi Minh colleagues, catching up on office gossip, project updates, and the places they were still exploring. Her fingers itched to book a flight every time she saw a picture of a hidden alley café or a street market bursting with lanterns. She began building her own travel bucket list, fueled by both nostalgia and desire. The travel itch had returned - fierce, urgent, undeniable.

One Wednesday night, the buzz of mid-week freedom had her clinking glasses at Imperfecto, their favorite rooftop haunt in Gurgaon, with her girlfriends Adira and Sia. Fairy lights tangled in the rafters above, the music throbbed low, and their table was cluttered with half-finished cocktails and fries they swore they wouldn't eat.

"I want to plan an international girls' trip," Magh said suddenly, twirling the straw in her mojito. "My first ever girls' trip overseas."

Without missing a beat, Sia raised her glass. "Cheers to that! What better day to plan it than ladies' night, and what better place than Imperfecto? So ironic, it's perfect," she laughed, eyes twinkling.

Adira leaned forward, curious. "I'm in. But where?"

Magh, always in savings mode, smiled. "Budget trip. While coming over, I saw an Air Asiana ad - roundtrip to Kuala Lumpur, fifteen thousand rupees. Big green letters. It felt like a sign."

Instantly, both phones came out.

Adira, the planner, methodically pulled up flight aggregators and travel blogs. Sia, the party magnet, started searching for rooftop bars near Petronas Towers. Within ten minutes, Adira exclaimed, "We could even take a road trip to Singapore! It's just a 7-8 hour bus ride. This itinerary looks doable."

"Two countries in one trip? Yes, please!" Magh said, her voice rising with excitement.

"Wait, now we're adding Marina Bay Sands to the list?" Sia chimed in. "This is becoming a proper trip."

Three different energies sparked across the table: Magh, the dreamer; Adira, the spreadsheet-queen; and Sia, the heartbeat of any party.

By the time the DJ switched to mellow closing songs, their flights were booked. And a month later, the trio touched down in Kuala Lumpur.

The week that followed was a montage of motion: Morning markets, afternoon rooftops, street food that left fire on their tongues, and souvenirs stuffed into every inch of their suitcases. They hopped across landmarks, posed under Twin Towers, danced through Sentosa, and clinked glasses under starlit skies.

At the departure gate, tired but glowing, Magh stared at her boarding pass and whispered, "I'll come back again."

The girls sat sipping coffee. One nodded. "For sure."

The other laughed. "I've seen enough here. Next stop? Someplace else. The world's too big, and we have too little time to live."

Back in her cubicle the next week, reality had returned, but Magh felt changed. She found herself listening more intently during the company's Global ARC Program - a mosaic of stories from colleagues stationed across continents.

Over lunch breaks and post-session mingles, she heard about London, Singapore, Melbourne, Toronto, and Tokyo. Each voice stirred something inside her. Vietnam had cracked open a door. Now she wanted more.

By the next day, she was browsing the internal careers portal. A seed of possibility was planted. She applied to a handful of global roles-quietly, with hope. But weeks passed. No response.

Then, one Friday, the office buzzed with farewell chatter. Harit had found a job in Vietnam at another company. He came back to wrap up his things and treat his colleagues on his last day. Magh stayed back for the low-key drinks in a Cyberhub bar called Social, where he shared his story.

"I applied everywhere," he said, sipping neat whiskey. "I got rejected everywhere too. But I didn't stop. I contacted people on LinkedIn, tailored every resume. Eventually, someone replied. That's all it takes-one reply."

Magh, chewing on her peri-peri wings and sipping her Tequila Sunrise, listened without blinking. She said nothing, showed no hint that she was feeling the same. But inside, her resolve tightened like a knot.

That night, in the cab ride home, she made a to-do list:

Message 10 people on LinkedIn every day. Don't give up.

One month later.

Wednesday, May 25, 2019.

Still curled under the covers, Magh debated - cab or metro or drive? The eternal morning question. She finally got ready, hair in a loose bun, and sat across from her father at the breakfast table.

Her mom served hot besan chilla and steaming masala chai while her father flipped the newspaper.

"I've been so busy with work these days," she said casually, stirring sugar into her tea, omitting the part about job hunting. Just then, her phone buzzed.

A LinkedIn message.

Heart racing, she opened it with her left thumb, chai in her right.

"Sure, let's connect on Skype. Send me your resume. – Vikram Oberoi, Partner, ARC, Singapore."

A smile lit up her face.

"What happened?" her dad asked, eyebrows raised.

Her mom, ever the romantic, chimed in: "Are you talking to a boy?"

Magh smirked. "I'm not telling you now. But when I do, you'll be the first to know obviously. Just pray Guruji listens."

Reena, being spiritual, immediately turned to the family temple and began muttering a prayer. Ashwani, always teasing, repeated his classic line:

"Jaag ke kario, bhaag ke nahi."

("Fall in love with your eyes open. Don't run away blind.")

Magh chuckled, pushing her chair back.

"It's not always about finding a guy, Dad. You already know I am focusing on building my career first that lets me see the world. Wish me luck for that. Don't always think about my marriage. See you in the evening."

She grabbed her laptop bag, flung her car keys into her hand, and walked out.

The sun was rising, soft gold spilling across the street. The world was calling again - and this time, she was prepared to step out of her comfort zone.

One and a half hours later, she pulled into the office parking lot. Unusually, her car ride had been quiet - no chatter from the radio, no news, no morning show hosts filling the silence. Instead, Ik Onkar, her favorite spiritual track, had played on a loop. It was her anchor, her compass when thoughts ran deep. And today, her mind was anything but still.

By the time she reached her desk, the morning chaos around her had blurred into the background. She powered on her laptop, opened her LinkedIn inbox, and found the message she'd been thinking about replying to during the drive.

She took a deep breath, steadied herself, and typed a thank-you note. It was simple and signed 'Sincerely, Grateful'. She acknowledged his response and expressed her enthusiasm about joining the Singapore team. With practiced confidence, she attached her freshly updated resume, a brief summary of her aspirations, and hit send.

For a moment, time slowed. A small smile tugged at the corners of her lips. It wasn't a leap, but it was a step - and it was hers. A quiet sense of accomplishment washed over her. She had taken initiative. She was steering her life in the direction she envisioned.

But dreams, she'd learned, were delicate things.

She closed the tab, grounded herself, and turned to her to-do list. The present still demanded her full attention. Lessons from the past had taught her not to place all her hopes on a single thread - especially one tied to a distant future.

This time, she would be smarter. She would explore opportunities abroad, yes, but not at the cost of her current work. Balance was the key. One foot in the now, the other edging toward what could be.

For two weeks, silence.

Magh barely noticed it at first; her calendar was packed, and her mind even more so. Work deadlines blurred one day into the next. But late at night, just before shutting her laptop, she'd find herself staring at her inbox, refreshing it. Once. Twice. Nothing.

She'd sigh, shut the screen, and convince herself, 'It'll come when it comes.'

Then, on a quiet Friday evening, just as she was about to call it a week, her screen lit up.

A new email from Jaron, the HR lead, popped up in her outlook with the Subject: Magh Mehra's Job Application - ARC Singapore

Her heart skipped a beat. She clicked it open.

Hey Magh, shall we connect on Monday morning to discuss your job interest that had been referred to me by Vikram?

Short. Simple. But it made her pulse quicken.

Without hesitation, her fingers flew across the keyboard.

Hi! Yes, absolutely. Monday morning works perfectly. Looking forward to speaking!

Jaron responded within minutes, blocking her calendar with a meeting invite.

As she hit Accept, a small smile spread across her face.

Her phone buzzed - a message from her team. "Drinks tonight?"

She hovered over the reply for a moment, then tossed her jacket over her arm and headed toward the exit.

"Not tonight," she muttered to herself. "I've got something to prepare for."

Less than a month later, Magh would look back on that quiet Friday evening and realize - it had been the beginning. Not loud. Not grand. No signs from the universe or fireworks in the sky. Just a simple message and a shift in her breath. But sometimes, beginnings don't come wrapped in noise. Sometimes, they arrive like a whisper.

From that Monday onward, everything began to move quickly.

The first round was the HR round, with Jaron himself. A calm conversation, more about alignment than interrogation. Still, her palms were clammy beneath the desk. She had rehearsed every possible question the night before, her notebook scribbled with bullet points and scribbled-out thoughts. But in the end, it was her instant thoughts that carried her through. She spoke with a quiet conviction that came from years of doing the work - of showing up, of leading silently.

When the confirmation came-"We'd like to move forward"- her breath hitched. Then it steadied. One down.

The second round felt heavier. A panel. Technical. Strategic. They threw scenarios at her like curveballs, and she caught them with the kind of calm that surprised even herself. She spoke less from preparation and more from experience. They asked her how she would handle a crisis. She answered by telling them about one she'd already lived through during her projects in Vietnam and Mumbai. No embellishment. Just the truth.

After that call, she closed her laptop and sat in silence. Not from exhaustion - but from the strange awareness that something was shifting. The email came the next morning: You're through to the final round.

She blinked at the screen, let the words settle, then smiled.

The third round was with Vikram. A husky voice on a Teams call and a man in his forties with a personality that seemed strong and straightforward. More vision than detail. He wanted to know not just what she could do, but who she was. What drove her. What she saw when she looked ahead to moving to Singapore. And Magh, for the first time in a long time, allowed herself to speak from that deeper place. Not the resume version of herself. But the real one - the one who had quietly built her way here, without shortcuts, without noise.

She closed that final interview with a simple "thank you" - and for the first time in weeks, she meant it. There was no lingering doubt, no second-guessing. She had given everything, and now, all she could do was wait.

Three weeks of silence followed. Days that dragged on, each one a reminder that, no matter how hard she had tried, nothing was certain. She told herself it was fine - not to worry, not to hope too hard - but the truth lingered like a shadow in her thoughts.

And then, on the morning of her birthday, the phone rang. The call from Jaron came in softly, almost hesitant.

It was an offer.

She didn't cry. Not yet. She didn't scream or jump or do any of the things she'd imagined she would do in that moment. Instead, she stood perfectly still, her fingers gripping the edge of the phone as if anchoring herself to the ground. The weight of it settled over her, quiet and heavy, like a promise she didn't know how to carry.

It wasn't until later, when she walked to her parents and handed them the letter, that the floodgates opened. Her father, his eyes twinkling with pride, gave her a gentle pat on the back. "The best birthday gift anyone could have," he said, his voice thick with emotion.

But all she could do was cry.

She didn't know if it was the relief, the joy, or the sheer exhaustion that finally broke through - maybe a mix of all three - but for the first time in weeks, everything felt real. And for that one fleeting moment, the future didn't seem so uncertain anymore.

Is this real?" she pondered. She asked her sister Ichha to pinch her to make her believe.

And then, quietly again, she smiled. Because what had started with a short call had become something more. A doorway. A leap. A new chapter.

P.S. She was ready.

CHAPTER 8

OLD SCHOOL, NEW CURRICULUM

Two months later, Magh stood at Indira Gandhi International Airport in New Delhi, surrounded by suitcases stuffed with her mother's homemade snacks, and the weight of a thousand unspoken emotions. Her ARC India colleagues, especially Saranya, had come to send her off. It was a progressive discussion when she had mentioned the ARC Singapore offer to Navneet. He was happy and extremely proud of her. He cleared all internal gates for her and eased her path to step into her dream world.

At the departure gate, her mother clung to her hand, eyes brimming with tears. "I am just going for two years, Mom. It's just a few hours away. As soon as I settle in, I will call you there. I can't stay without your food. For how long will I eat burnt food haha," Magh chuckled, trying to sound braver than she felt. "It's a temporary work vacation just like Mumbai or Vietnam. I'll be back before you know it."

Her mother's smile wobbled, her eyes shimmering as she tried to stay strong. "I know, beta… I'm so happy for you. But you're still my little, clumsy Magh." Her voice cracked, and she cupped Magh's face gently. "I'm going to miss you so much. Even if you come home late by a few minutes, I start worrying. And now, sending you so far away…" She paused, swallowing back tears. "My heart is not ready. But I want to support you. I know you'll give this everything you have." Her grip stayed firm, as if letting go would make the moment real.

Magh's father stepped closer, clearing his throat as he discreetly brushed the corner of his eyes with the back of his hand. He wrapped her in a tight hug - one that said everything he couldn't. "Go live your dream, Magh," he murmured, his voice thick. "Do wonders out there. You've always made us proud." He pulled back just enough to flash a crooked smile. "And don't worry about your mom. I'll take care of her. We'll come to visit soon. I'll start saving more…" He chuckled softly. "I'll even cut down on my drinks - at least, I'll try."

She nodded, swallowing the lump in her throat, and turned towards the entrance, her trolley rattling ahead of her. With every step, Ichha took quick snapshots on her phone - trying to capture the chaos, the love, the sadness… everything.

Ichha walked beside her and stopped at the gate, dramatically placing a hand on her chest. "This is it," she whispered, then nudged Magh with her elbow. "The moment your life begins… and the moment I finally get full custody of the room." She let out a mock sigh of relief. "Please go and conquer the world quickly, okay? So I can enjoy all the cupboard space in peace. I've already planned where my shoes will live."

She pulled Magh into a quick side hug. "But seriously… go make magic. I'll miss you - but not the mess you leave on the bed."

Behind them, Sia and Adira stood in silence, their eyes red. When it was time to part, they hugged Magh fiercely.

"You settle in first," Sia said, her voice cracking. "We're booking our flights to Singapore the moment you give us the green light."

"Promise us you'll start having the best time of your life and stop overthinking for no reason," Adira added, wiping her cheeks.

Magh managed a smile through the tears. "Only if you two come soon."

And with one last look back, she stepped forward into the unknown - carrying their hopes, her dreams, and the quiet strength of every goodbye.

Her journey into a new life had begun long before takeoff - but as she stepped into the towering double-decker A380 of Singapore Airlines, her heart skipped a beat. It was her first time on such a grand aircraft, and the premium economy seat her new office had arranged felt like a quiet nod from the universe: This is real. You're moving forward.

As the plane soared into the sky, leaving behind the familiar chaos of Delhi, Magh curled into her window seat, wrapped in a soft airline blanket. Outside, the world looked peaceful - clouds stretching like an endless sea below her.

She stared out for a long time, lost in a whirl of thoughts. Her life had always been full of people - she was the girl who never did things alone, who found comfort in company, who had grown up sheltered, in a cocoon woven from family, familiarity, and quiet rituals.

But this - this was different. This was her, on her own, flying toward a life she hadn't dared to imagine a few years ago.

She thought back to how it had all unfolded - almost like a divine plan, carefully designed: her self-exploration during the Mumbai project. The solo trips she hesitantly took, her understanding of the meaning of freedom, and her first international assignment in Vietnam, which had seemed daunting but ended up being a turning point.

It all made sense now.

Those chapters were never detours; they were stepping stones, pieces of a larger picture that only now came into focus.

She let out a soft laugh, shaking her head at the memory of how heartbroken she'd been when she didn't get the Cape Town project, and how she'd cried over it like it was the end of the road.

But here she was - flying to Singapore, starting a new job, a new life. Something far bigger than she'd even known to dream of.

God really does know better. He always has a plan, she thought, pressing her forehead lightly to the window.

And somewhere, high above the clouds, Magh smiled - not just with her lips, but with the quiet peace of a heart finally understanding the journey it had taken.

Two weeks before Diwali, on the crisp morning of October 16, 2019, Magh finally landed at Changi Airport.

It was a small personal victory - she had missed visiting this airport on her last Southeast Asia trip, with flights routed through Kuala Lumpur instead. But this time was different. This time, she wasn't here as a tourist. She was arriving as a resident, an expat, a woman stepping into a new chapter.

The moment she stepped off the aircraft, something shifted. It wasn't loud or dramatic. Just a quiet flutter in her chest - a feeling she couldn't name, but couldn't ignore either.

She smiled without realizing it, her eyes wide as she took in the gleaming glass, the indoor gardens, the soothing order of everything around her. There was something about Changi - elegant, welcoming, impossibly efficient - that made her feel like the world had paused for a second just to let her catch her breath.

I can do this, she thought, the words repeating like a quiet mantra in her head.

A job I actually like. A whole new country to explore. A home not too many hours away. This feels right. This is right.

With that quiet confidence holding her steady, she collected her luggage and stepped into the tropical warmth of Singapore. The ride to the hotel blurred past her in a haze of thoughts and light fatigue.

She checked in, called home to let everyone know she had arrived safely, and then - finally - collapsed onto the soft bed.

That night, under the hush of unfamiliar city lights, she drifted into sleep.

Not with anxiety. Not with fear.

But with the gentle hum of possibility, and the fragile, beautiful dreams she had just begun to knit in this new world.

The next morning, Magh woke up with a smile that reached her eyes.

There was something quietly thrilling about it - her first day in a new city, a new job, a new life. As she buttoned up her crisp white shirt, blue pants, and ran her fingers through her hair, she laughed to herself. This feels like getting ready for the first day of school.

She grabbed a quick breakfast downstairs in the hotel, surrounded by other guests in suits, the quiet murmur of business meetings in the background. Everyone seemed to be chasing something. So was she - but it felt different. She wasn't chasing anymore, maybe just for one day, but she felt lighter.

The cab ride to the office was short, but every turn through downtown Singapore felt like a page out of a dream she had once dared to imagine. The skyline gleamed under the morning sun, and her heart beat a little faster as she approached her new workplace.

And then, there it was.

Bold. Familiar. Comforting. ARC.

She saw the same letters she had once walked under five years ago in India. But this time, they were in bold black and yellow letters, on a new land, in a new chapter.

She paused at the entrance, heart full.

It was like life had come full circle-but in a way that said: You've grown, and you're ready to embark on a new journey.

And with that thought, she stepped forward, ready to begin again-but this time, as a version of herself that only she knew she had become.

It wasn't just any job - it was the same consulting world she knew, but in a new geography: a new curriculum, a new version of her old world.

Within a week of joining, she was handed a new project. She spent her days trying to understand her new managers and adjust to the rhythm of this old, yet new workplace. Some days felt long and draining; others passed in a blur. It wasn't like her time in India, where colleagues felt like family and leaders were just a conversation away. Here, everything seemed to be in place - the role, the structure, the opportunity - yet she still felt far from settled, as if she had everything but hadn't quite found her place.

Three weeks in, she visited her first client site - a government office - for a workshop alongside her partner Vikram who had recruited her. She was marking the kickoff of the project with him that day. As she stepped off the bus and walked toward the building, memories of home came rushing back. The clean walkways, clear signage, and automated gates reminded her of how structured and efficient things could be in a developed country. There was beauty in the order, and for a brief moment, she felt a sense of calm.

Inside the elevator, she spotted the client. With a warm smile, she waved hello. To her surprise, the client didn't smile back - just a nod, cool and distant. It caught her off guard. A little confused, she chose not to dwell on it. People here may take time, she reminded herself. Give it time. I'll find my rhythm. I always do.

As Magh stepped into the meeting room alongside her partner, Vikram, she offered a polite greeting to the client, Mr. Jon Chew - a man of average height, dressed sharply in a black business suit, his expression unreadable. She had hoped that this time, unlike their previous interaction in the elevator, he might return her greeting with a smile. But once again, he barely acknowledged her.

Just as they were about to take their seats, Jon glanced around the room and said, flatly, "Looks like we're one chair short. Since you're two minutes late, the others have taken the seats."

Magh instinctively checked her watch: 8:32 am. A wave of discomfort tightened in her chest. Two minutes late? she thought. Is that really such a sin? She recalled the frustrating five-minute wait for the elevator and five minutes to wait for his team member downstairs to escort them upstairs, but brushed the thought aside, forcing herself to focus. The meeting had begun, and Jon's Mandarin-accented English required her full attention.

Vikram stood tall, his posture relaxed but unmistakably commanding. With a well-built frame, neatly tailored shirt with the sleeves rolled, and salt-and-pepper hair that only sharpened his charm, he had the kind of presence that didn't demand attention - it earned it. Behind dark-rimmed glasses, his eyes held a focused intensity, calm but alert, like someone who'd mastered the art of reading a room before speaking. When he finally did, his voice was steady, composed. "Jon, it would really help if we could get a personal access card next time - that way we can bypass the admin desk and reach on time," he said - not a hint of blame, just quiet precision.

Magh glanced at her director, pleasantly surprised. Most leaders she'd heard about in Singapore would've simply apologized and moved on. But Vikram had chosen to speak up - not to blame, but to improve things. She couldn't help but smile softly, her lips curling with quiet gratitude.

Jon responded with a stiff nod and an exaggerated expression. "Sure. Since it's your first day, let's move on to the agenda."

The meeting proceeded. Vikram presented confidently, covering every detail. When he wrapped up, Jon turned to him and said, "Let's set up another meeting next week to begin the project."

They stood, shook hands, and then Jon walked over to Magh. This time, he extended his hand, offered a small smile, and said, "Good work."

For a moment, the chill of the morning melted, and Magh allowed herself to feel proud-not just of the work, but of the team she was stepping into.

As they stepped out of the client's office into the warm midday light, Magh walked a few steps beside Vikram before asking, a hint of hesitation in her voice, "Are clients always this strict here too?"

Vikram let out a soft laugh, the kind that made the tension of the moment feel smaller. "People are different everywhere, Magh. It's not really about the location. What matters is how we adapt-how we read the room, manage the situation, and present our point in a way that builds understanding for the future. You need to start learning this art soon. Here, you won't have much hand-holding, you have to learn to manage such situations on your own."

Magh nodded, a thoughtful smile tugging at her lips. "That's true. I'm starting to see that. Slowly, but surely."

Just then, their cab pulled up. They got in, and the conversation drifted into silence as the city blurred past the windows. Soon, they were back at the ARC office, ready to carry on with the rest of the day.

The client eventually awarded the project to their firm, and just like that, Magh found herself committed for the next six months - alongside her partner, Vikram, three junior team members, and a new intern.

This wasn't just another assignment. It was different - the kind where no manager hovered over her shoulder to double-check slides or cushion a difficult client conversation. This time, her name stood on the line. Her decisions. Her delivery. Vikram supervised the project, yes, but only from a distance.

He was different from Navneet.

Navneet had shaped Magh in her early years - steady, supportive, the kind of boss who guided her through the messiness of consulting with patience and reassurance. He had been her safety net.

Vikram, on the other hand, operated with a different energy altogether. He expected her to deliver from experience, not instruction. No hand-holding, no protective bubble - just open ground, real stakes, and opportunities waiting to be claimed. With him, the training wheels were off. It was her turn to ride on her own.

Magh knew this was the stretch that could push her from "Senior Consultant" to become a Manager. She'd already had the conversation - clear milestones, expectations, and timelines. And she was ready. Or at least, she told herself she was.

She always had the heart of a lion - classic Leo, ambitious, proud - but deep down, her risk appetite was cautious, careful. The kind that took small steps toward the unknown while secretly wishing to leap.

Then came Chenxi Chew.

She walked into the meeting room behind Vikram, a petite 21-year-old with chestnut brown hair pulled into a lazy ponytail, dressed in business casual that still held the air of a college student. "This is Chenxi," Vikram said briskly. "She's joining us for two months from the University of Hong Kong. Magh, get her settled, assign her a few light tasks to begin with."

And just like that, the baton was passed.

Magh nodded, trying to mask the flicker of panic behind her polite smile. Manager. That word echoed in her head. Was this how Saranya or Taran had felt when they first led her?

"Chenxi," Magh said, standing up. "Let's grab a coffee before we dive in. I'll walk you through a few things."

The girl smiled eagerly and followed her down the hallway to the pantry.

As the two sat down with cups of Kopi Kosong in hand, Chenxi leaned forward, brushing her hair behind her ear.

"So," she asked, "how long have you been with ARC?"

Magh took a sip, the bitterness grounding her nerves. "Five years," she said, clearing her throat. "Started in India. Just moved here about four months ago."

Chenxi blinked. "Five years? That's like... a lifetime in consulting. Most people barely make it past two , I heard!"

Magh laughed, a little surprised by the girl's candor. "Yeah, I get that a lot."

"So what keeps you going?" Chenxi asked, genuinely curious.

Magh looked at her for a moment. And in that brief pause, her mind flashed through late nights, tight deadlines, the thrill of cracking client problems, and the quiet pride of being trusted - finally.

She smiled, the corners of her lips curling with both honesty and pride. "I guess somewhere between the chaos and caffeine," she said, "I started falling in love with this fast-paced world. Every day throws something new at you. You're constantly stepping into unfamiliar zones, figuring things out as you go. But every time I come out the other side, I've learned something and grown. That thrill - it keeps me going."

Chenxi took a sip of her coffee, watching her thoughtfully. Then, with a small nod, she said, "That's really inspiring. I'm excited to learn from you."

The words landed softly, but their weight lingered.

For the first time, Magh didn't just feel senior by designation - she felt it in her bones. It wasn't about job titles or slides with her name on top. It was the quiet recognition of experience, of having been through the trenches long enough to guide someone else through them too.

The thought followed her back to her desk and stayed with her all afternoon. What kind of manager would she become? Would she morph into the kind she'd once struggled under - distant, buried under layers of pressure, letting that stress cascade down onto the team? Or could she be like Taran, like Navneet - leaders who had kept their calm even when things cracked at the seams, who had shielded their team while pushing them to grow?

She wasn't sure yet. But one thing she knew: she had the choice. Everyone has a choice.

P.S. Point to be noted, readers!

And perhaps, this project wasn't just a client deliverable - it was her first real test of becoming the kind of leader she worked with.

Three months into the project, Magh had stumbled more than once. Difficult client conversations, tight deadlines, and late-night team calls had become the new normal. But with each challenge, she grew stronger. She learned when to push her team, when to defend them, and, just as importantly, when to step back and reflect.

Jon Chew was a classic micro-manager - constantly hovering, questioning, and escalating even the smallest delays. He made her work harder, yes - but also made her think sharper. She didn't always win the battles. There were moments when her team felt the heat she couldn't shield them from. And she carried that with her.

But in those moments, she often found herself thinking back to Navneet - her mentor and former leader in India. One of his lessons echoed in her mind:

"A real leader doesn't pass down pressure. They absorb it, filter it, and give their team clarity - not chaos."

The day Jon escalated an issue over a one-hour delay in deliverables, she paused. She remembered Navneet's words, took a breath, and chose not to let the heat ripple down to her team. Instead, she sat with them, asked for ideas, and navigated a path forward - together.

Over time, she started building her own leadership compass. She created a personal "repository" of learnings from her time in India and from observing strong leaders in Singapore. In every tough situation, she paused for a few seconds and asked herself, "What would the good ones do?" Not always perfectly, but piece by piece, she began crafting her own leadership style - blending her instincts with lived experience.

Each day brought a new twist: team conflict, client tension, or simply the crushing fatigue of back-to-back calls. But as the project neared completion, the pressure hit a new high. Late nights became routine. Still, Magh made it a point to protect her team's spirit. She organized casual dinners, quiet coffee breaks, and even some late-evening walks - anything to remind them they were more than the sum of their deliverables.

She remembered how she had once been on the receiving end - when managers passed the stress down like a hot coal. She had promised herself she'd do better.

When the six-month-long project finally wrapped, an unexpected email arrived. It was from Jon - short, curt, typical of him:

"Thanks, Vikram. Your team did a good job."

She was CC'd.

That was it. No fanfare. But those few words felt likc a trophy. Recognition from someone who rarely gave it meant more than paragraphs from someone who often did.

On the final day at the client site, Magh turned to Vikram and the team and said, "Drinks are on me." It was time to celebrate. Not just the project delivery, but the cocktail of experiences they had all weathered together.

Down the road, at a cozy bar called Happy High, the team finally let go. Laptops stayed shut. Laughter replaced deadlines. For one evening, they were just people, not roles. And with Monday just around the corner, they knew a new challenge would come - but tonight, they celebrated resilience.

During the celebration, between clinks of glasses and laughter echoing off the bar walls, Chenxi turned to Vikram with a thoughtful look in her eyes. She raised her voice slightly to be heard over the music and asked,

"Vikram, can I ask you something? As a partner and such a senior leader, what advice would you give to an intern like me who wants to grow and one day become a successful leader like you?"

It was a question that was both simple and deep-one that cut through the noise of the evening.

Magh, wrapping up her second round of sangria - her go-to celebratory drink - caught the question and instinctively turned toward them. She smiled. The moment felt familiar. A few years ago, she had been the one asking such curious, wide-eyed questions. In Chenxi, she saw a younger version of herself.

Vikram, sipping his scotch on the rocks, chuckled and leaned back in his chair. He took a thoughtful pause before answering.

"You know," he began, swirling the ice in his glass, "every leader eventually finds his or her own style. There's no single formula. What worked for me may not work for everyone - but here's what I learned along the way."

"In my early years, I said yes to everything. Big tasks, small errands - didn't matter. I saw every task as a learning opportunity. And I don't regret that. It helped me build a solid foundation."

He paused again, his eyes reflecting both nostalgia and wisdom.

"But over time, I started burning out. My productivity dipped. I was stretched thin. That's when I realized - saying yes to everything doesn't make you efficient, it just makes you exhausted. It taught me one of the most important lessons: the value of prioritization."

Magh leaned in slightly, quietly absorbing every word. She wasn't taking notes on paper, but she was etching every line into her memory.

"When I became a manager," Vikram continued, picking up a truffle fry and smiling faintly, "I learned the difference between being busy and being effective. Delegation became essential - not just as a task, but as a mindset."

"Delegation isn't just assigning work. It's an art - to delegate the right things to the right people. And that art can't be faked. If you don't master it, you may become a manager, sure - but not a leader. That's a different game."

He looked at Chenxi, his tone both firm and kind.

"To grow, you need curiosity, judgment, and the patience to learn from failures. A calm mind, a sharp eye, and the ability to lift people up, not wear them down-that's what will take you far."

Chenxi nodded slowly, clearly impacted by the wisdom in Vikram's words.

Magh raised her glass toward Vikram in a silent toast of gratitude and inspiration. She knew this wasn't just a casual bar conversation-it was a moment. One of those rare ones that stay with you long after the music fades.

As Vikram wrapped up his final words, Magh stood, glass in hand, her smile bright and unwavering.

"To us," she said, voice clear and steady. "To this team, to a successful go-live… and to many more wins ahead."

Laughter rose. Glasses clinked. And for a moment, the room shimmered with something more than celebration - something earned.

Later, on the quiet bus ride home, Magh leaned her head against the window, watching the city slide by in blurred lights and half-memories. Every moment from the past weeks began to play back: the chaos, the breakthroughs, the quiet support from Vikram, the fierce dedication of her teammates, the unexpected kindness of clients. Each interaction had left a mark, a lesson, a quiet nudge forward.

By the time she reached her co-living flat, her heart was full, tired, but full. Her roommate greeted her with two spoons and a tub of leftover dessert. No words needed. They shared the sweetness in companionable silence.

Later, under the soft hum of the ceiling fan, Magh slipped beneath her sheets and closed her eyes. Sleep took her fast, deep, and complete - as if the night itself had promised her a pause, as if tomorrow could wait.

A few months later, during the next appraisal cycle, Magh got promoted to manager.

The title felt heavy, not just with responsibility, but with stories.

She had watched from the sidelines for years, learning, unlearning, observing managers from India to Singapore.

Now, the view had shifted. And she knew power didn't come with a manual. Leadership, as she would soon learn, was less about answers and more about navigating the grey zones.

But before all the lessons, came the moment. And she celebrated it in the most Magh way.

The first call she made was to her mother.

"Mom… I became a manager," she whispered.

There was a soft gasp on the other end, followed by a wobbly, breathless silence.

"Arre, beta…what a good news. Congratulations. Thank you Guruji. I love you beta," her mother finally managed, voice trembling with pride. In that instant, both of them laughed through tears, happy tears, tired tears, victory tears. This milestone belonged as much to her family as to her.

Her father took the phone next, clearing his throat like he hadn't been secretly listening the whole time.

"My daughter… a Manager!" he declared, chest swelling. That night, he celebrated in his own simple way, by pouring himself an extra drink and raising an imaginary toast to the girl who carried her dreams like fire.

Later, Ichha called after finishing work.

"Amazing, sister! Now buy me an iPhone, okay?" she teased before bursting into giggles.

Magh rolled her eyes. "No iPhone, but at least now I can help finish the home loan faster," she said, knowing exactly what this promotion meant to her family.

"You're our support system," Ichha replied softly. "Always have been."

She sent a quick update to Navneet, just one line, but enough for him to understand what this meant. His reply came instantly: Knew it. Proud of you.

And to seal the day, she joined an impromptu video-call e-party with Adira and Sia, the three of them cheering, laughing, and pretending their mismatched mugs were champagne flutes.

The real journey wasn't the promotion.

It was what came after.

But in that night full of calls, tears, laughter, and tiny celebrations, Magh allowed herself to feel it -

She had earned this.

And this was only her beginning.

CHAPTER 9

HOLDING THE WHEEL

"Am I ready?"

The question pulsed in Magh's mind like a heartbeat, steady and insistent, as she sat across from Vikram in the sunlit conference room. It was a quiet Tuesday, but everything about the moment felt louder, brighter than usual.

Outside the glass walls, the office moved at its usual weekday rhythm. Keyboards clicked softly in the background, the distant whirr of the coffee machine came and went like a sigh, and someone was laughing near the design pod, their voice muffled through partitioned walls. The scent of fresh filter coffee mingled with the faint chemical sharpness of whiteboard markers.

Magh wore a navy-blue blazer over a crisp white shirt, sleeves neatly rolled up, hair pinned back to keep her thoughts clear. A pair of understated gold studs glinted as she turned her head. Vikram, on the other hand, looked as he always did - calm, pressed, and slightly too relaxed for the intensity of what he was about to say. His grey jacket hung off the back of his chair, sleeves of his pale blue shirt rolled to his elbows, a thin silver watch catching the morning light.

The conference room itself was glass-walled and minimal, punctuated only by a sleek wooden table, a shared notepad, and a half-finished cup of decaf cappuccino from Starbucks at Vikram's elbow.

Vikram leaned back slightly, fingers lightly interlocked. His tone was polite, almost casual, as if he were discussing weekend plans instead of handing over the reins.

"This time, I won't be involved in the day-to-day," he said evenly. "No check-ins. No steering."

He paused, letting the silence settle just long enough to make its weight felt.

"I'll just be a listener," he added, a faint smile tugging at the corners of his mouth. "But this time, it's your show to run for the next year."

The words landed with quiet finality.

Magh managed a small nod, even a smile - but something inside her shifted.

It felt like the ceiling above her had vanished; the sky suddenly infinite.

No fallback. No shadow to stand in. No doors to knock on when the wind picked up.

This wasn't a rehearsal anymore.

She was at the helm now, fully exposed, fully responsible.

And the realization was both electrifying and terrifying.

Somewhere in the space between the adrenaline and the uncertainty, it clicked:

The cockpit was hers now.

Magh cleared her throat, steadying her voice.

"Sure, Vikram. I'm ready to lead this project - and I'll make sure I prove that this promotion was earned. I know it wasn't an easy decision. The competition was intense, and I don't take it for granted. I'll lead this project with focus and accountability. I've absorbed a lot over the last few months - every feedback, every challenge - and I'll put that learning to use when it matters."

Vikram smiled, the kind that softened his usual seriousness.

"Don't treat it like a battle, Magh. There's no scoreboard to beat here. You don't need to prove yourself every single day."

He leaned back in his chair, letting his words land gently.

"Think of it more like a badminton match - my favorite game for a reason. The shuttle keeps flying back and forth. Sometimes, the opponent smashes hard, and you scramble. Other times, your own partner misreads the play. That's how it goes."

Magh's shoulders relaxed slightly as she listened.

"You'll drop a few points. We all do. What matters is how quickly you recover and stay in the rally," Vikram said, tapping the table lightly for emphasis. "Don't panic. Don't try to win every shot. Just stay in the game. Respond, don't react. That's how you build rhythm."

He paused. then added with quiet conviction,

"You'll make mistakes, everyone does," Vikram said, his tone steady, almost calm. "But as a manager, you won't get the luxury to make many. You'll have to cover your team's missteps, take responsibility for what goes wrong. It will scare you at first, losing the safety net above you, but that fear is exactly how you'll learn. That's how you grow."

Where Navneet had guided her gently through every misstep, Vikram empowered her to step up and navigate the storm on her own.

Magh nodded slowly, her expression firm yet thoughtful. She extended her hand across the table.

"Thank you for trusting me, Vikram," she said, her voice steady. "I've worked under a few tough managers in the past - some who micromanaged every move, and others who had a stronger approach - the good managers, like you. I've learned a lot from both, but now I want to craft my own journey. I want to lead with a mindset shaped by those lessons and not just replicate what I've seen."

Vikram chuckled softly, shaking her hand with an easy grip. He leaned back in his chair, arms loosely crossed, the corners of his eyes crinkling.

"There's no such thing as a 'good manager,' in my opinion," he said, with a shrug. "That label's too simplified."

Magh tilted her head, curious.

"What really matters," Vikram continued, "is having a balanced approach. Leadership isn't about ticking boxes or trying to be everyone's favorite. It's about showing up with clarity and empathy, especially when things go sideways."

He paused, glancing toward the glass walls where the rest of the team buzzed around, oblivious to the quiet mentor session taking place.

"Someday," he said, "you might have to ask your team to stretch. Stay late. Rework something for the third time. It'll feel uncomfortable, but that won't make you a bad manager. What matters is how you ask. Will you demand it? Or will you lead with humility? That's what separates the leaders people follow willingly from the ones they merely obey."

Magh was silent for a moment, absorbing his words. They weren't just professional advice, they were lived experience, passed down with intention.

"Every tough situation will ease up, eventually," Vikram went on, more softly now. "What lasts is how your team feels through it all. If they trust you, if they know you've got their back, not just for the deliverable, they'll work with you, not just for you. That's when the magic happens."

He leaned forward, elbows resting on the table.

"Remember, you don't have to know everything, or get everything right the first time. You just have to listen, stay grounded, and respond instead of reacting. That's how you grow and that's how you help your team grow too."

Magh felt a quiet surge of clarity. She wasn't just stepping into a new role - she was stepping into a new identity. One built not on authority, but on awareness.

"I'll remember that," she said, her voice softer but more certain. "And I'll try to lead the way I wish I'd been led and always to step into the shoes of my previous roles to better assess the situation."

Vikram smiled, nodding with satisfaction.

"That's all I needed to hear."

Outside the glass, the world continued - emails flying, footsteps rushing past, the low hum of focused energy. But for a brief moment inside that room, it was just a passing of the torch, from one leader to the next.

Magh drew her chair back, gave Vikram a composed smile, and stood.

"Thanks again for trusting me," she said, her voice steady but touched with quiet emotion.

"You'll be fine," Vikram replied, giving her a knowing nod. "You just don't know it yet."

With that, she turned and walked out of the room, her mind already shifting gears.

The open-plan office hummed with the soft white noise of a Tuesday afternoon - keyboard clicks, low murmurs, the occasional ding of a Teams notification. Magh moved through it with purpose, weaving past glass cabins and soft-seating pods until she reached her desk. Her corner overlooked the corridor leading to the breakout area, bathed in natural light. She slid into her chair and opened her laptop.

Her fingers hovered over the keyboard as she created a new meeting invitation.

Subject: Briefing on ADA Project

She stared at it for a moment. It sounded too formal. Too heavy. She deleted it.

Subject: Catch-up on ADA Project

She smiled. It felt lighter. Warmer. Like a gentle nudge instead of a command. A subtle but intentional shift.

First lesson in motion, she thought. From theory to practice: tone matters.

By the time the afternoon sun began dipping slightly west, Magh had gathered all the relevant inputs from the client. She had a decent understanding of expectations, timelines, and initial priorities. It was time to align the team.

She reserved a glass meeting room on the 17th floor, one that overlooked the iconic Marina Bay Sands skyline. The view was a showstopper, calming yet powerful, as if reminding everyone inside of both the scale of the city and the possibilities ahead.

She arrived a few minutes early. When she opened the door, five faces turned toward her.

Harry, Derek, and Chenxi, familiar faces from her previous project, gave her small, respectful nods. The other two were new interns: Lily, shy but observant, and Regine, bright-eyed and slightly nervous.

To her surprise, all five of them stood up as she entered, like students greeting a teacher.

She froze for a second, not expecting the gesture. It felt foreign. Formal. Almost hierarchical.

She smiled, disarming the moment.

"Hey, hey - no need to stand. This isn't a classroom," she said with a soft laugh, raising her hand as if waving off a ceremony.

Everyone relaxed, exchanging slightly sheepish smiles.

"We're one team here," she continued, walking to the head of the table. "There's no hierarchy when it comes to respect. Age, designation - it doesn't matter. What matters is that we treat each other with openness and support. We'll face some tough milestones on this project, and the only way through is together."

A light energy returned to the room. The air, which had been stiff with formality, now began to loosen. Someone made a joke about the cafeteria running out of cutlery again, and laughter followed. For a few minutes, the group shared snippets of their day - how the post-lunch slump was kicking in, or how they'd lost track of time working on something small but oddly complex.

Magh allowed the chatter, listening with half a smile. Then, gently, she brought the focus back. She opened her laptop and shared the project deck on the screen.

Over the next twenty minutes, she walked them through the core objectives of the ADA project, the expected deliverables, stakeholder map, and tentative timelines. She explained roles, not as assignments handed down, but as contributions woven into a collective goal. Questions were asked. Ideas shared. Notes taken. The meeting felt more like a dialogue than a directive.

As the session wound down, the team began packing up.

But Chenxi lingered.

She closed her laptop slowly, then looked up at her with a thoughtful expression.

"Hey Magh," she said, "can I ask you something?"

She paused, curious. "Of course, go ahead."

"How does it feel, to be a manager now?" she asked. "I mean… I hope I get there one day too."

Magh blinked, caught slightly off guard by the question. She smiled, the weight of it settling in.

"It feels… good," she said after a pause. "But it's different. There's a sense of responsibility I'm still getting used to. In many ways, I'm still the same senior consultant I was last month. I have the same desk and same team. But the weight has shifted. The eyes are different. The expectations are wider."

She folded her arms, leaning gently against the edge of the table.

"It's like wearing new shoes, they fit, but I'm still learning how to walk in them without stumbling. The real change isn't in the title-it's in the decisions you're accountable for, and the way your words start to carry more weight than you realize."

Chenxi nodded, quietly absorbing her response.

"I look forward to working closely with you again," she said. "I think I'll learn a lot. I feel like our paths might be somewhat similar."

Magh chuckled, soft and genuine.

"You will learn, Chenxi, sometimes from people, sometimes from mistakes, and most of the time, from how you handle the things no one prepared you for."

"Thanks, Magh. Have a good day," she said, picking up her notebook and walking out with a small smile.

She watched the door close behind her.

The room was quiet again. Only the soft hum of the air conditioning and the fading light of the afternoon remained.

Magh turned toward the window, her eyes tracing the lines of the skyline. Marina Bay reflected the mellow tones of the sun, still strong but beginning to soften.

Life really is a circle, she thought. The same questions I once asked my seniors - I'm answering now.

And in that quiet moment, something in her settled.

This was just the beginning - but it already felt real.

After the meeting, Magh stepped out for a quick coffee break. The late afternoon sun cast long shadows across the breakout lounge, where a few others were half-typing, half-chatting, cradling mugs of caffeine like anchors.

She made herself a strong cup, no sugar, and walked over to the quieter corner by the tall window. Her phone buzzed with unread messages, but her thumb instinctively opened her favorites list and tapped Mom.

The moment her mother's voice came through, warm and familiar, Magh felt something inside her unclench.

"Tell me everything," her mom said. "Don't skip the tiny details."

And so she did.

She poured her heart out - about the meeting with Vikram, the nervous interns, Chenxi's question, her own uncertainty wrapped in responsibility. Her voice started out firm, recounting events with precision, but slowly began to crack around the edges.

Her mother listened patiently, letting her speak without interruption.

Then came the sentence that broke her.

"I wish I could still hear all your jibber-jabber in person," her mom said softly. "Over chai and those sandwiches you love… like the old days."

That did it.

Magh turned her face toward the window, blinking fast as tears welled up. She tried to speak, but her throat tightened.

"Mom… don't," she whispered, her voice shaking. "I'm already overwhelmed. If you say things like that, I'll cry right here in the middle of the office."

Her mother chuckled gently. "Then cry. You're still my girl. Even if you're a manager now. I am sure even managers have a heart and cry in front of their moms."

Magh laughed through her tears, wiping the corner of her eye with her sleeve.

"You're coming next month anyway. So start packing. And don't forget to bring your homemade chai masala. We'll sit and talk all day like we used to, okay? It'll be nonstop nonsense and your famous unsolicited advice."

"I'll bring extra," her mom said, smiling through the phone. "You'll need it."

They said their goodbyes, hearts full but heavy. As Magh ended the call, she stared at her reflection in the glass, coffee in one hand, phone in the other, eyes still slightly damp.

A manager… and yet, still a child.

She exhaled slowly, letting the truth of that thought sink in.

Maybe everyone has both sides, she mused. Even the toughest managers I once feared probably had their own vulnerable corners, little children tucked somewhere beneath the armor of KPIs and authority.

She sipped her coffee, now lukewarm, and looked back at her day. The handshakes, the team meeting, the skyline, Chenxi's question, her mom's voice - each moment stitching itself into something new, something forming.

The journey had begun, and it was already deeper than titles.

A month later, she booked a flight for a short trip to Thailand. The plane ride to Bangkok had felt like a jailbreak. After weeks buried under cascading deadlines, overlapping time zones, and milestone meetings that bled into midnight, Magh had finally drawn a hard line: three days, just three days to disappear on a long weekend.

Her rooftop seat at Breathe, an upscale bar tucked into the 40th floor of a Sukhumvit tower, felt like the first breath after drowning. The late morning sun bathed the terrace in gold, and below, the city swirled in organized chaos - motorbikes darting between tuk-tuks, street vendors calling out, and temple bells faintly echoing somewhere in the distance.

Magh exhaled and tilted her head back, letting the warmth soak into her skin. A tall glass of her go-to cocktail Sangria, glistening with condensation, stood before her.

She reached for it -

Buzz.

Her phone vibrated once, then again. The screen lit up with a new subject line on her Outlook app:

"URGENT - ADA Escalation: Security Breach"

She blinked.

Her fingers tightened around the glass without lifting it. The words on the screen blurred for a second as her pulse picked up. She tapped it open.

The client's message was crisp. Cold. The kind of formal that stings. A sensitive folder - containing financial summaries and sensitive data - had been downloaded from the client's secure drive the night before. Traced back to her team. Labeled: Chenxi's IP address and email ID.

A flash of heat rose through her spine.

No. Not on this trip. Not now.

Then another ping.

Chenxi had already responded to the client informally, with a line-and-a-half apology, without context, and without escalating to her first.

Magh's stomach dropped. She could already hear the subtext: lack of control, immature team, compliance risk.

She set her drink down slowly, untouched. Her lips were dry. She stood, walked to the terrace's edge, and dialed.

The phone rang once, then again.

"Chenxi?" she said, low and calm.

There was no greeting. Just breathing. Then a cracked voice: "Magh, I-I'm sorry. I didn't mean to… I swear, I thought I was backing it up for Monday's sync. It was late; I was tired. I didn't know it was flagged. I didn't even know it was sensitive - Oh God. Am I going to be let go?"

Magh clenched her jaw. Part of her wanted to scream. The other part - the one trained in client crises - took over.

"Chenxi. Listen to me. We can't change what's happened, but we can control how we respond."

Silence.

She took a breath and softened. "First, step away. Five minutes. Walk around your room. Drink some water. Cry if you need to. Then come back. But I need you to be clear-headed."

She let out a breath that sounded like a sob. "Okay."

Her other phone buzzed. A Teams message from Vikram:

"Magh, be on top of the escalation. This client is very important to us. We can't afford to lose its trust in us. I know you can handle it."

She stared at the message for a long second. Her hand stopped shaking.

She remembered her own client escalation years ago. The fear, the 3:00 am. insomnia. And Taran, her manager at the time, who had taken the heat without flinching.

Now it was her turn to wear the armor.

Back on the line, she said, "I'm drafting a formal response. I'll take accountability. But from now on, if something even feels off - you come to me, before the client, always."

"Yes. I understand," Chenxi whispered.

"And Chenxi?" she added. "Mistakes happen. What matters is how you rise from them. You're not going to lose your job. But you need to own this moment. Not fear it."

There was a pause, then a quieter, steadier: "Okay. Thank you."

"Good. We'll sync in an hour. I want you to prepare everything, your access logs, screenshots, steps taken. We'll build a timeline, identify the breach point, and close this down cleanly. One step at a time."

She hung up.

The glass of cocktail still glistened, untouched, now slightly watered down by melted ice. The city was still buzzing below, but her day had shifted from vacation mode to crisis response.

Magh picked up her phone again, opened her Outlook app, and started typing the details to prepare a formal acknowledgement email.

Her fingers flew across the screen. She wasn't just documenting the event - she was containing it.

One hour later, Magh sat in silence as the clock ticked past 6:30 pm. The hotel room was dim, the only light spilling from her screen. The night had the eerie stillness of a storm waiting to break. She took a sip of lukewarm chamomile tea when a message pinged on her laptop.

Chenxi: Hi Magh. Draft incident report attached. Please let me know if it requires any modification. Apologies again for my mistake.

She clicked.

The document opened slowly, like a curtain rising on a stage she wasn't ready to watch.

At first glance, it looked neat. But as her eyes traced the lines, something began to feel… off.

She squinted.

The attached video footage of deletion history was blurred, nearly unusable.

The title was spelled wrong. "Incedent" Report.

Timestamps: jumbled and contradictory.

Critical logs: missing entries.

Her fingers hovered above the keyboard.

This wasn't just sloppy. It was dangerous.

In any data breach scenario, documentation is the lifeline - the only proof to show what happened, when, and how it was handled. If this went to the client as is, they were setting themselves up for legal exposure.

She leaned back in her chair, eyes closed briefly.

Old Magh - fresh out of her first promotion - would've fired off an angry reply by now. But that version of her had learned the hard way that anger only adds fuel to a fire.

Instead, she reached for her bottle of water. One sip.

Then another.

She looked out the window. Bangkok's skyline blinked back - so alive, yet tonight, it felt like all eyes were on her. She had almost forgotten that she was on her planned vacation. She was virtually in office and physically on this long-awaited planned vacation.

Then she called her.

"Hi Chenxi," she said, steadying her voice like an anchor. "Can you share your screen with me?"

Her voice came on, shaky and low. "Uh-sure, just a sec…"

The screen shared. Her cursor hovered nervously. Magh could almost hear her heartbeat through the line.

"Alright," she said gently. "Take five minutes and go through the report again. I'm on the call. Just... look at it with fresh eyes."

She started scrolling. A minute in, she heard her voice shiver.

"Oh... the spelling..." she muttered. "And that's the wrong timestamp... and the link - it's the old footage. I am so sorry. I have been making so many mistakes since yesterday. What is wrong with me? I really need to calm down, please help me, Magh, I never make such mistakes."

She didn't react. She just let her process.

"It's okay," she said, finally. "I spotted a few more. Want me to walk you through them?"

She nodded, swallowing hard.

"You're making more mistakes because you're panicking, Chenxi," she continued, her tone softer now. "And that's understandable. But right now, panic is our enemy."

There was silence.

"I just didn't want to mess it up," she whispered.

"I know," she replied. "But when things go wrong, we don't fall apart; we pause, accept it, and move into action. That's what separates a team that survives a crisis from one that implodes under it."

She hummed yes, slowly, the words sinking in.

"Give me one more hour," she said. "I'll fix it all, I promise."

"Good. But this time, it needs to be clean. We won't get a second shot."

She was about to end the call when her inbox lit up again.

Subject: Re: URGENT - ADA Escalation: Security Breach

Her eyes darted to the sender.

Jon Chew, the name known to all.

She clicked.

The email was short, but sharp, each word like a bullet:

"I didn't expect it. Such a reckless mistake. I want a full review tonight. Late call. My calendar holds only one slot - 11:30 pm. No other."

Magh stared at the screen. Her heart gave one solid thud.

Still on call, Chenxi noticed her voice change.

"What is it?" she asked. "Is it… really bad?"

She didn't speak immediately.

"Magh?" she pressed. "Am I… going to get fired?"

Her eyes stayed locked on the screen, mind racing. She inhaled slowly.

"Chenxi," she said, voice calm but edged with steel, "don't jump to conclusions. No one is talking about firing right now."

She fell silent.

"Let's not think about the worst-case scenario. Our job right now is one thing: damage control. No panic. No guesswork. Just facts and protocol."

"But what if-"

"No 'what ifs' tonight," she cut in gently. "We prepare. We walk into that 11:30 call with every single detail. Every log, every version history, every correction noted. And we show it was a unintentional error."

She paused.

"We take control of the narrative. And we do it together."

Chenxi exhaled sharply, like someone surfacing from deep underwater.

"I'll fix the report. I won't let you down. I know you are on your vacation and I spoiled it all. I am extremely sorry."

She nodded. "No need to apologize so many times, Chenxi. Let's handle this as a team. You have one hour to update the report. Then we regroup. I will grab a quick dinner; you should also have your dinner."

She ended the call and leaned back in her chair again. Her phone buzzed with yet another Teams ping. She didn't check.

Instead, she stared at the ceiling, her mind rehearsing every possible question that could come from Jon.

The clock read 11:10 pm.

The world outside Magh's window was asleep, but her mind was wide awake. The city lights of Bangkok blinked faintly in the distance from her hotel's windowsill, reflecting in the glass like a warning signal. Her laptop fan hummed steadily, keeping rhythm with the thud of her heart.

She sat ready.

Calm posture. Screen clean. Tabs aligned.

A shared folder sat open: final incident report, corrected footage, team logs, data history - every breadcrumb was accounted for.

The corrected draft had finally come in from Chenxi after another two sync-ups during her dinner. Sloppy had become solid. Panic had turned to precision.

She messaged her a quick line:

"Thanks. Rest now. I'll take it from here."

She replied with another long message of apologies.

Now, her cursor hovered over the blinking link:

Join Microsoft Teams – Security Escalation Review

11:30 pm. She clicked.

The screen is loaded.

A minimalist home office appeared. Stark white walls were present. A single scroll painting hung behind the desk - calligraphy, likely a proverb.

Jon appeared on screen wearing a neatly buttoned black shirt, his new thin-framed glasses, and eyes that missed nothing.

He nodded once. "Good evening, Ms. Magh. I appreciate you taking the call at this time. But I didn't expect this situation from a team representing such a big firm."

His tone was firm, but clipped - like silk over steel.

"I hear you Jon," Magh responded. "My apologies for this situation and thank you for having this call at this hour."

"I assume you already know the concern," he said. "The first response from Chenxi to the incident was informal and... disappointing."

He paused for effect. "And vague."

Magh kept her face steady. "Yes, I fully acknowledge that. The initial response did not meet the expected standard, and I take responsibility for responding out of panic."

Jon raised an eyebrow. "That's a strong word. Responsibility."

"Yes," Magh replied. "Because while a junior analyst promptly replied, I am her manager. I should have set the escalation protocols with the team before it reached you."

He said nothing more, but clicked audibly - no doubt opening the report.

"I've uploaded the detailed incident report," she continued, "with corrected footage, time-stamped logs, and a full trace of our internal handling. The document includes system scripts, team escalations, and all information linked to the deletion event."

Jon's eyes scanned off-screen. His fingers tapped lightly on his desk. The room remained silent - but intensely so.

Finally, he spoke.

"I see the details. This shows clarity. The event appears to be internal human error. No breach of external systems."

"That's the depth of the situation," Magh confirmed. "No customer data was compromised. The deletion occurred due to a misconfigured script scheduled without proper version control. It has since been corrected, peer-reviewed, and a new dual-approval protocol has been implemented."

Jon looked back at the screen.

"You understand," he said, voice measured, "in our culture, we treat every data incident as a loss of face. Even if the data is safe, perception matters."

Magh nodded slowly. "I do. And that's why I'm not here to make excuses. Only to present facts, take accountability, and share what actions we've already taken."

There was a pause. A long one.

Then Jon closed the folder on his end. The tapping stopped.

"You seem calm, or are you pretending to be, because you know I can pull back from this project based on this incident?" he said, almost curious.

"I am learning from some of my leaders that panic leads to poor decisions," she replied. "And one meaning of leadership is about offering clarity when everyone else is drowning in confusion. I am still a learner every day, learning from leaders like you."

He gave a single nod, eyes narrowing.

"I'll review this in more depth tomorrow. If no further gaps are found, I will consider the issue resolved. However-"

He raised one finger, "-We will expect tighter quality control from now on. No more surprises."

"Understood and noted, Jon. You have my word."

A small smile tugged at the corner of his mouth.

"You're different from many of the project managers. Keep learning from Vikram," he said.

"I intend to."

He nodded once more. "Good night, Ms. Magh."

"Good night."

The screen dimmed.

Magh exhaled slowly, allowing her body to sink into the chair.

No one clapped. No music played. But something had shifted.

The storm had passed - for now.

She poured the last of her chamomile tea into a cup and stared at the rising steam.

Leadership, she realized again, wasn't about showing power. It was about absorbing the impact - and still thinking clearly.

The steam from her tea curled upward, vanishing into the night. Magh stared into the cup, her face expressionless, not from lack of emotion, but because she was processing.

The call had gone better than expected.

She knew how rare that was.

In most escalation calls, especially with stakeholders like Jon, the tone rarely softened. Their approach was deeply rooted in discipline - a misstep wasn't just a technical issue; it was a reputational wound. The fact that he'd smiled, even slightly, meant something.

Her phone buzzed.

Chenxi: Hey, still on the call?

Magh typed slowly, her fingers finally relaxing.

Magh: Just ended. It's under control. Jon will do a detailed review tomorrow. But no alarms for now.

A typing bubble flickered, then stopped. Then it returned again.

Chenxi: I am still very scared about my job. I am worried that legal action might be taken against me.

She stared at the screen for a long second before replying.

Magh: You made mistakes, yes. But we all do. I have done many things and sometimes I still fail even if I give my best. But we have to learn and make things better together as a team. Communicate at the right time and something that even I am learning every day is staying calm in a storm and focusing on the actions.

A long pause.

Chenxi: I'll never forget this. I owe you a lot for keeping me calm and helping me to sail through this.

She smiled faintly and replied,

Magh: Just don't make me regret it.

Then, she closed the laptop - but her mind didn't power down with it. She curled up in bed and then it was a constant battle of swirling thoughts.

Five Years Ago – Flashback

Magh sat in a noisy cafeteria, her ID badge swinging nervously as she tapped her foot against the chair leg. Across from her,

Sia looked pale, on the verge of tears.

"I swear I didn't mean to," Sia whispered. "I just clicked the wrong workflow and the data got cleared."

Magh's heart was thudding. Back then, she wasn't a manager. She wasn't even a lead. But she was the loudest in the room.

"You what? Do you realize what you've done?" she'd snapped, voice rising. "You've just deleted a full day's sales records! You didn't think before clicking? Are you even serious about this job?"

Sia had gone silent. People at nearby tables had turned.

Later that day, Magh found out that the auto-backup had saved everything. The panic? Unnecessary. The yelling? Unforgivable.

Her manager, Taran, had called her aside quietly.

"You were right to be concerned," he had said, "but you handled it like someone lighting a fire in a room already filled with smoke."

That moment never left her.

That night, she had apologized to Sia.

And slowly, she started learning what real leadership meant.

Present – 12:40 am

Magh stood up, her legs stiff from hours of sitting, and walked to the window. The city blinked back - glittering, indifferent - while behind those lights, a thousand battles like hers were quietly unfolding.

She thought of Chenxi - her steady voice during chaos.

Of Jon - stern, but fair in ways that counted.

She was once impulsive and loud, brittle like glass. Now, she was quieter and clearer. She was not perfect, but learning to pause before she cracked.

Her phone buzzed again.

[Vikram, 12:41 am]: Thanks for holding it all together today, Magh and Chenxi. Jon said the team handled it well. Good work, but I don't want any such mistake to happen again.

She stared at the message for a moment, then typed back:

"Couldn't have done it without all of you. Thank you for being the backbone."

As she curled into bed, the tension in her spine slowly uncoiled. She wasn't done - far from it. There would always be another escalation, another deadline, another voice too loud in a meeting.

There would be people who would talk without empathy.

They would micromanage without context.

Undermine without reason.

But there would also be those who stayed late on calls.

They sent quiet check-ins.

They let her fail, but not fall.

"One fire down," she whispered to herself. "Tomorrow, we walk through another. Not alone."

She turned off the light.

P.S. Because in the end, the corporate world didn't just teach her to survive pressure. It taught her who makes it worth surviving. And that lesson? She would carry it - long after the fires were out.

CHAPTER 10

STIR, SIP & REPEAT

Two years later.

The ballroom lights at The Royals in New Delhi shimmered softly as guests began to pour in. The invitation had said it simply:

"Join us for Magh & Karam's Cocktail Party : Let's raise a toast before we tie the knot."

And somehow, that line felt more poetic than formal. Magh's journey had begun in boardrooms, had escalated through deadlines, had survived late-night calls, and today… it had arrived at a cocktail party. Full circle.

As Magh and Karam entered the warmly lit venue, she felt something inside her. Not peace, no, she was never fully peaceful - but a comforting sense of arrival.

Karam held her hand, steady as always.

He was a gentleman in every sense, calm when she spiraled, composed when she overthought, sporty and sharp, and the steady anchor to her hyperactive chaos. On their first date, he understood that her mind often raced faster than her thoughts. He knew even then, that he had to be her calm in all the overthinking and chaos. As a corporate banker, Karam carried a sense of balance in his professional journey. He knew how to draw boundaries between his personal and professional life. He failed at times, but he never gave up on this goal.

He understood her corporate madness without getting sucked into it.

He didn't compete with her shine; he protected it.

Tonight, he looked at her as if she were the entire room.

Navneet stepped in with the same calm authority he carried into every strategy meeting. But today, his eyes held warmth - real warmth.

Vikram walked in with Chenxi, wearing his usual half-smile, hands tucked in his pockets as he observed the room before joining it. He had just finished a work call and was updating Chenxi about it. Chenxi was taking notes and helping Vikram cover for Magh's time off. Even with all the deadlines, they had managed to fly to India for Magh's wedding. They just couldn't miss it.

Saranya, Taran, and Sia arrived together, laughing like the old team walking into one more project war room.

Her parents and her sister Ichha greeted guests at the entrance , glowing more than any chandelier in the hall.

Magh wasn't sure when she started smiling, but she realized she hadn't stopped.

They all gathered around the center bar, a circular counter, just like the metaphor they had lived through.

Ichha lifted her glass first.

"To my little sister and our new family member Karam. Welcome to our crazy family. My sister is your problem from now on haha," she chuckled.

Everyone laughed and Magh laughed a bit more as the memories of all her sibling fights flashed quickly in her head.

As the party continued, a few drinks later, everyone started gravitating towards their own comfort groups.

The corporate counter was as expected; Magh & Karam joined them for the next round at the table where all Magh's office friends were gathered.

They both joined in and clinked their glasses.

Navneet raised his glass to give his toast.

"To the new world they're stepping into," he said, nodding at Magh and Karam.

"And to the worlds we all built along the way."

Glasses clinked.

A sound that felt like closure and beginning in the same breath.

They settled at a round table, the same people who had once crowded around office desks, projects, whiteboards, and screens. Only today, no laptop glowed between them.

The conversations began naturally, overlapping, soft, nostalgic.

Vikram leaned back, shaking his head.

"I remember when Magh was terrified of handling her first client escalation in Singapore."

He smirked.

"Now look at her. Running projects all by herself. With another one from now on, the marriage project. He laughed as he took a sip of his drink."

The table burst into laughter.

Karam looked at Vikram and broke into a big laugh. He clinked his glass with him in agreement.

Chenxi. still the enthusiastic junior, chimed in,

"Honestly, every time Magh led a call, I felt like - okay, this is how grown-ups do it."

She blushed when everyone laughed.

"But now when you are on your marriage leave and I am talking to clients directly, I hear your voice in my head sometimes, Magh."

Taran shook his head dramatically.

"My life turned out peaceful after you left the team. No 10:00 pm messages that say 'one quick thing'."

Saranya jumped in,

"Oh please, Taran. You miss the chaos. Admit it. Dude, you were a great teammate and of course I miss you every time I have our favourite masala chai in the office.

He shrugged.

"...a little."

Magh walked to Saranya, gave her a tight side hug and just stood by her. She knew that if she went deeper down memory lane, she would break into tears.

Sia took the spotlight next, her eyes glowing with pride.

"Life changed for me too. I'm running my own business now.

It was the best decision I ever made. But today I can share the worst part.

I can't blame a manager anymore when things go wrong."

The table roared.

Navneet watched the group like a man witnessing a timeline unfold.

He finally said,

"Funny how careers look so similar on paper but feel like cocktails - layers, mixes, surprises. We all have our own journeys, yet we have one thing in common. We didn't give up on our journeys in chaos. We all found our own ways to come through it. Magh found her way to Singapore. I can never forget her sad face when Cape Town didn't work out.

He looked at Magh.

"It all happened for a reason; otherwise, how would you have met Karam?" he chuckled.

Everyone laughed.

"You are so right Navneet, I thank my stars all the time for the decisions I made that once sounded like a mistake. I don't regret any of my decisions now." Magh added.

She looked at Karam softly and laid her head on his shoulder.

Karam, holding her hand under the table, whispered,

"It's so good to see you smiling when you're with your people."

She whispered back,

"They built me."

He smiled, brushing his thumb over her hand.

"And I'll carry you forward."

In that moment, she realized something -

he was her calm after every corporate storm,

her balance,

her grounding,

her home.

The conversations grew deeper, looping between the past they shared and the futures they were stepping into.

No one spoke like colleagues anymore.

Tonight, they were just people…people who had survived deadlines, celebrated wins, cried in bathrooms, chased promotions, found courage, and somehow ended up here…

At a cocktail party for a girl who turned her chaos into a story.

Magh looked around the ballroom -

the Partners who trusted her,

the friends who stood by her,

the junior who grew with her,

the woman who reinvented herself,

the family who believed in her,

and the man who brought out the best in her.

And she felt it.

This wasn't an ending.

Just a new bar, a new drink, a new beginning.

She raised her glass.

"To the people who made me."

"To the stories we lived."

"And to the ones we'll mix next."

Clinks echoed again - soft, warm, final, and hopeful.

The last pour of this chapter.

The first pour of the next.

ONE FOR THE ROAD

Ten years. A full decade.

Magh often found herself repeating those words, not out loud, but quietly, as if testing whether they felt real. The years had flown by, yet each one had left its distinct imprint - messy, meaningful, and full of movement.

When she began her career, Magh didn't have a five-year plan or a fancy roadmap. What she did have was curiosity, caffeine-fueled ambition, and a quiet fire to prove to herself that she belonged in rooms her family didn't expect her to enter. What she didn't have - yet - was perspective.

That came with time. And trial. And a long list of missteps that slowly turned into lessons. Along the way, she arrived at some important learnings - things I believe you, dear reader, will find worth exploring now that you've come this far:

The Power of Choice

Corporate life, she had realized, is both a mirror and a maze. It reflects who you are when no one's watching, and it twists and tests you until you learn how to navigate with your own compass.

Magh had seen people rise fast - brilliant, magnetic, impossible to ignore. She had also seen others lose steam, undone not by lack of skill, but by the weight of unchecked burnout.

The difference? Often, it came down to choice.

Every day in the corporate world presents a buffet of choices - how you respond under pressure, how you treat the colleague who underdelivers, whether you chase credit or focus on contribution.

Magh didn't always get it right. She had snapped in meetings. Stayed silent when she should've spoken. But with every mistake came a quiet reckoning - and a better choice the next time.

One lesson stood out: emotional resilience is not about suppression; it's about precision. Feel, process, then respond with intention.

A Lesson She Carries

There was a time, early in her career, when Magh worked under a manager and the client who made her question herself daily. Communication was vague, feedback was laced with condescension, and expectations kept shifting like sand. For weeks, she spiraled. She googled other jobs. She doubted whether she was cut out for this at all.

And then - one late evening, after another confusing conversation - she paused and asked herself:

"What if this is the training ground, not the test?"

Such moments made her an observer of day-to-day corporate experiences. Not with detachment, but with intent. She noticed how her manager worked with senior leadership, how they chose their words under stress, how they maneuvered through chaos.

What had felt like sabotage slowly became a silent mentorship in stakeholder management, political navigation, and the art of staying grounded.

It was one of the hardest stretches of her career - and one of the most formative.

Growth Isn't Comfortable

One of the biggest myths Magh had unlearned was that growth feels good.

It doesn't - not always. Sometimes it feels like being stretched too thin, like failing in front of people you admire, like showing up tired but still showing up.

Corporate life doesn't promise clarity or fairness. It gives you ambiguity, deadlines, brilliant minds, messy systems, and the occasional meeting that could've been an email.

But within that mess is where growth takes root - quietly, stubbornly.

Magh had learned this: your real resume is built in the moments no one sees - when you take the blame you could deflect, when you speak up though it shakes your voice, when you keep going without the applause.

Leadership Before the Title

Magh didn't wait for a title to lead - and she'd seen too many who had titles but never truly led.

Leadership, she had come to believe, is not a role. It's a posture: a series of quiet choices that stack up to influence and integrity.

She remembered the intern who asked the most thoughtful questions in a room full of seasoned professionals. Or the analyst who held the team together during a messy product launch, without being asked.

These were leaders - not because of where they sat on the org chart, but because of how they showed up.

Leadership begins the day you stop waiting for permission.

To You, Dear Reader

If you've made it here, Magh sees a bit of herself in you. Maybe you're just starting out. Maybe you're at your own decade mark. Maybe you're somewhere in between, trying to decide whether to push through or pivot.

Wherever you are:

You have more power than you think.

You may not control your organization chart or your skip-level manager. But you control how you show up - how you think, how you lead, how you grow.

- You can choose to make hard things teach you.
- You can choose character over convenience.
- You can lead without a mic or a mandate.

Magh's journey is far from over. If anything, this book is just a checkpoint - not a finale, but a pause between chapters.

There will be more pivots.

More pressure.

More lessons wrapped in mistakes.

But also more quiet wins. More clarity. More moments that remind her why she chose this path in the first place.

Before she steps into her next fire, she leaves you with this:

Where are you on your journey?
What decisions - loud or quiet - are shaping your professional self and the person you're becoming?

What kind of legacy are you building in meeting rooms, late-night emails, or quiet resilience no one sees?

Your story won't look like hers. It shouldn't.

Whether you're an intern learning the ropes, a mid-level manager balancing chaos in industry or in consulting, or a C-suite leader still figuring it all out, this message is for you.

This is your corporate cocktail.

Own it. Stir it. Spill it. Spill it again.

But never stop learning from it, because each sip, each mistake, each success is part of the recipe.

It's messy, it's complex, but it's always evolving.

And here's the thing we remind ourselves every day:

We always have a choice: to respond, to push boundaries, to adapt, to evolve, to begin again.

Because in the end, the greatest cocktail isn't the one you drink - it's the one still getting stirred or shaken, with a little bit of grit, a dash of ambition, and a whole lot of courage.

So, what will you add to yours?